THE PROPHET OF MODERN CONSTITUTIONAL LIBERALISM

John Stuart Mill is the father of modern liberalism. His best remembered work, *On Liberty*, published in 1859, changed the course of the liberal tradition. What is less well known is that his ideas have profoundly influenced the American constitutional rights tradition of the latter half of the twentieth century. Mill's "harm principle" inspired the constitutional right to privacy recognized in *Griswold* v. *Connecticut*, *Roe* v. *Wade* and other cases. His defense of freedom of expression influenced Justices Holmes, Brandeis, Douglas, Brennan and others, and led to greatly expanded freedom of speech in the twentieth century. Finally, Mill was an ardent feminist whose last important work, *The Subjection of Women*, was a full-scale and, for its time, radical defense of complete gender equality. *The Prophet of Modern Constitutional Liberalism* is a book for lawyers who want to understand the intellectual origins of modern constitutional rights. It is also a book for political philosophers interested in the constitutional implications of Mill's conception of freedom.

John Lawrence Hill is the R. Bruce Townsend Professor of Law at Indiana University's Robert H. McKinney School of Law in Indianapolis, where he teaches constitutional law and legal philosophy classes. He holds a J.D. and a Ph.D. in philosophy, both from Georgetown University. He has published several books in law, ethics and philosophy.

The Prophet of Modern Constitutional Liberalism

JOHN STUART MILL AND THE SUPREME COURT

JOHN LAWRENCE HILL
Indiana University

CAMBRIDGE
UNIVERSITY PRESS

CAMBRIDGE
UNIVERSITY PRESS

University Printing House, Cambridge CB2 8BS, United Kingdom

One Liberty Plaza, 20th Floor, New York, NY 10006, USA

477 Williamstown Road, Port Melbourne, VIC 3207, Australia

314–321, 3rd Floor, Plot 3, Splendor Forum, Jasola District Centre, New Delhi – 110025, India

79 Anson Road, #06-04/06, Singapore 079906

Cambridge University Press is part of the University of Cambridge.

It furthers the University's mission by disseminating knowledge in the pursuit
of education, learning, and research at the highest international levels of excellence.

www.cambridge.org
Information on this title: www.cambridge.org/9781108485296
DOI: 10.1017/9781108755993

First published 2020

Printed in the United Kingdom by TJ International Ltd. Padstow Cornwall

A catalogue record for this publication is available from the British Library.

Library of Congress Cataloging-in-Publication Data
Names: Hill, John L. (John Lawrence), 1960- author.
Title: The Prophet of Modern Constitutional Liberalism : John Stuart Mill
and the Supreme Court / John Lawrence Hill, Indiana University.
Other titles: John Stuart Mill and the Supreme Court
Description: Cambridge, United Kingdom ; New York, NY, USA : Cambridge
University Press, 2020. | Includes bibliographical references and index.
Identifiers: LCCN 2019043917 | ISBN 9781108485296 (hardback) | ISBN
9781108719452 (ebook)
Subjects: LCSH: Civil rights--United States. | Civil rights--Philosophy. |
Mill, John Stuart, 1806-1873--Influence.
Classification: LCC KF4749 .H55 2020 | DDC 342.7308/5--dc23
LC record available at https://lccn.loc.gov/2019043917

ISBN 978-1-108-48529-6 Hardback

To my family

Contents

Introduction *page* 1

PART I MILL AND HIS PLACE IN THE LIBERAL TRADITION

1 Mill's Life, Work and Character 7

2 Liberalism before Mill 27

3 Inventing Modern Liberalism 38

PART II MILL AND THE CONSTITUTION

4 Constitutional Liberties before Mill 57

5 The Intellectual Origins of the Right to Privacy 77

6 Mill and Modern Freedom of Expression 100

7 A New Equality 120

Index 137

Introduction

The cemetery Saint Veran in Avignon, France, is a twenty-minute walk outside the walls of the old city, a short distance from the palace of the fourteenth-century popes and the river Rhone. Toward the back of the cemetery, inauspiciously nestled among the markers and mausoleums, stands a sepulcher of flawless white Carrara marble – the only one in sight without a trace of religious symbolism. It was here that John Stuart Mill buried his wife of seven years, Harriet Taylor Mill, after she succumbed to what Mill called "the family disease" – tuberculosis – in November 1858.[1] There is an old legend that the cottage Mill purchased after her death overlooked the cemetery and that Mill could look upon Harriet's grave from his window.[2] The legend is, as the cemetery caretaker described to me, "finely formed, but not fully true." The cottage was actually about a ten-minute walk from the cemetery. Nevertheless, Mill furnished it with the furniture from the room in the Hotel d' Europe where they had spent their last night together, and where Harriet had died.[3] For the remainder of his life, Mill split his time between London and Avignon, visiting her grave several times a day before joining her again in 1873.

Mill published *On Liberty*, the single most influential work of liberal political theory, three months after Harriet's death, in February 1859. This was the same year in which Tocqueville died and Darwin published his *Origin of the Species*. In the United States, the North and South were headed precipitously toward armed conflict. Two years earlier, in 1857, Chief Justice Roger Taney of the US Supreme Court had delivered his disastrous *Dred Scott* opinion, the very first Supreme Court

[1] John Stuart Mill, "Autobiography," in *Autobiography and Literary Essays as part of Collected Works of John Stuart Mill (hereinafter* CW*)*, ed. John M. Robson (Toronto: University of Toronto Press, 1978), vol. 1:240.

[2] Gertrude Himmelfarb, Editor's Introduction to *On Liberty* (Harmondsworth: Penguin edition, 1974), 24.

[3] Nicholas Capaldi, *John Stuart Mill, A Biography* (Cambridge: Cambridge University Press, 2004), 245–48 (describing the circumstances surrounding, and after, Harriet's death).

decision to recognize a constitutional right protected by the Bill of Rights. The right recognized, however, was the property right of slaveholders to own and transport slaves to the "free" territories in the United States. This decision led to the Civil War and to the subsequent adoption of the Fourteenth Amendment to the Constitution in 1868. The Fourteenth Amendment, in turn, inaugurated a new era of individual rights protections – protections which, a century later, came to take the form of the liberalism Mill had outlined in *On Liberty* and other works.

John Stuart Mill's place in the liberal tradition has been the subject of a vast literature a great deal of which views him as a classical liberal. He was not. Mill was the true prophet – and architect – of modern progressive liberalism. While he retained some of the assumptions of earlier classical liberals – particularly their distrust of government and their anti-paternalism – Mill offered an entirely new defense of liberalism. Where classical liberals had thought about liberty as a "negative" value – the absence of coercion or constraint by government – Mill connected liberty to the more "positive" values of autonomy, self-development and what we might call "self-individuation." Self-individuation itself required the discovery, development and expression of one's true self, including one's character, opinions, beliefs and plan of life.

This new conception of liberty would inevitably influence the way we think about what rights we have, how freedom can be infringed and how our Constitution should protect our basic liberties. His concept of freedom consists of three basic and interrelated ideas each of which has become central to our American constitutional tradition beginning, for the most part, in the 1960s. First, there must be a private sphere in which the individual is free to develop their own tastes, opinions, character and plan of life. Second, the individual has to be free to express his ideas, beliefs and convictions – not simply for the sake of others, but for the sake of his own self-actualization. Third, there must be equality – not simply the formal equality before the law defended by classical liberals and modern conservatives but, rather, as he put it in his Autobiography, an "equal freedom of development for all individualities."[4]

Mill's three principles – privacy, free expression and equality of condition – are the three notes in the chord of our modern constitutional rights tradition. The case announcing the right to privacy, *Griswold* v. *Connecticut*, was decided in 1965, just a little over a century after Mill defended his "harm principle" in *On Liberty*. *Griswold*, of course, led to *Roe* v. *Wade* and the right to abortion, *Lawrence* v. *Texas*, announcing a right of sexual autonomy to LGBT individuals and *Obergefell* v. *Hodges*, establishing a constitutional right to gay marriage. Mill is mentioned in some of these opinions: in one case, he is virtually plagiarized in an important concurring opinion on abortion rights by Justice Douglas,

[4] Mill, *Autobiography*, CW, 1:260.

occasionally he is directly quoted in a majority opinion, but much more frequently he is mentioned in the dissents, when a Justice wants to point out that the source of the principle adopted comes not from the constitution but from a nineteenth-century political thinker.[5]

Mill is probably best remembered among constitutional lawyers for his influence on our free speech jurisprudence. His intellectual impact on Justices Holmes, Brandeis and Douglas, in particular, is clearly discernible in their opinions and other writings. In fact, Holmes met Mill personally as a young man while on a visit to London in 1866. Holmes' and Brandeis' development of the "clear and present danger" test after World War I, the subsequent expansion of the First Amendment right to speak and publish things traditionally prohibited as "offensive" and the extension of freedom of speech principles to putatively false speech, as in defamation, all find their origin and clearest defense in Mill.

Mill's influence on modern equal protection jurisprudence is more submerged, refracted through the writings of so many more recent writers on racism and feminism. Yet he was the first to introduce a more substantive conception of equality into the liberal tradition. His writings on slavery and the American Civil War are less well-remembered today, yet when the Civil War broke out and public opinion in England was clearly on the side of the South, Mill defended the North in a series of newspaper writings and speeches that made him extremely unpopular in his own country. When his old friend, Thomas Carlyle, whose conservatism had soured with age into a reactionary anti-humanitarianism, published his "Discourse on the Negro Question," suggesting that the newly freed slaves in Jamaica were much better off under the yoke, Mill penned an impassioned rejoinder calling Carlyle's piece "a true work of the devil."[6] And when Lincoln was assassinated, Mill compared him to the greatest martyr to philosophy, observing that "the death of Lincoln, like that of Socrates, is a worthy end to a noble life, and puts the seal of universal remembrance upon his worth."[7]

Mill's feminism, moreover, was legendary. As a Member of Parliament, his speeches in defense of women's suffrage and to abolish such discriminatory provisions as the Married Women's Property Act were so radical for his time that he was frequently laughed at not simply by the Conservatives, but by members of his own Liberal Party. His last published book, *The Subjection of Women*, is the earliest and, still today, the best defense of liberal feminism. Yet for all this – and in contrast to the Supreme Court's privacy and freedom of speech jurisprudence – Mill is mentioned nowhere in the Equal Protection context. Yet, as we will see, many of his

[5] See, for example, Chief Justice Roberts dissenting opinion in *Obergefell* v. *Hodges*, 576 US —, 135 S. Ct. 2584 (2015) discussed in Chapter 4.

[6] Mill, "The Negro Question," CW, 21:95.

[7] Mill to Cairnes (May 28, 1865), CW, 16:1057.

most incisive and pragmatic points in *The Subjection of Women* anticipate, in detail, Supreme Court decisions in the context of gender.

Crucially, Mill insisted that it is not simply *government* which constitutes a potential threat to liberty, but *society* as well. Informal social forces – tradition, custom, habit, age-old prejudices and the "tyranny of the majority" (a term Mill so profitably borrowed from Tocqueville) – infringe individual freedom by cutting the individual off from sources of self-discovery and self-development. This move was pivotal, even fateful, for liberalism because it set up the central tension in modern liberalism: Since freedom requires limits on government power but also requires that government have sufficient power to counteract the sources of private power, modern progressive liberalism inevitably involves a balancing act between less government and more – both in the name of freedom. What distinguishes Mill from twentieth-century progressives is that, in his practical conclusions, he typically erred on the side of less government whereas they normally err on the side of more.

It is genuinely ironic that many contemporary lawyers are, at best, only vaguely aware of the name, John Stuart Mill. It is still more ironic that many judges and even most Justices of the Supreme Court should have carried on Mill's mission, often unwittingly, casting his ideas into the form of constitutional rights without a clear sense of their origin. But this should not surprise us. Judges and lawyers are "practical men," not philosophers. Though trained in the common law, they sometimes mistake for real tradition what John Maynard Keynes called "the voices in the air" that come from the theorists of a previous generation.[8] Whether they know it or not, it is Mill's voice which they so frequently have been channeling.

In his classic work on the history of liberal thought, L. T. Hobhouse wrote that the essence of liberalism is "the belief that society can safely be founded on the self-directing power of human personality."[9] Mill's work epitomizes this belief – indeed, this faith. Though it is seldom recognized today, no other political thinker has had as profound an influence on our recent constitutional rights tradition. If there is anyone worthy of the title "the prophet of American constitutional liberalism," it is an Englishman, John Stuart Mill.

8 "Practical men, who believe themselves to be quite exempt from any intellectual influence, are usually the slaves of some defunct economist [or philosopher.} Madmen in authority, who hear voices in the air, are distilling their frenzy from some academic scribbler of a few years back." John Maynard Keynes, *The General Theory of Employment, Interest and Money* (London: MacMillan, 1936), 383.

9 L. T. Hobhouse, *Liberalism* (1911), 66.

PART I

Mill and His Place in the Liberal Tradition

1

Mill's Life, Work and Character

I never meant to say that the Conservatives are generally stupid. I meant to say that stupid people are generally Conservative.[1]

EARLY YEARS AND EDUCATION

John Stuart Mill was born in London on May 20, 1806.[2] He was born into one of the most influential intellectual circles of all time. His father, James Mill, was a close friend and collaborator with Jeremy Bentham, the apostle of utilitarianism. Bentham was already famous, having published his *An Introduction to the Principles of Morals and Legislation*, the groundwork for utilitarianism, during the 1780s. James Mill himself would later gain fame for writing important books on economics, the theory of mind and a history of India. Their intimate circle included such luminaries as the economist, David Ricardo, who had been a neighbor of the Mills, and John Austin, the first important legal positivist in the Anglo-American tradition.

There can be no other way to think of the circle into which Mill was born than as an assemblage of great minds thoroughly committed to overthrowing the old moral and political order. Bentham, the elder Mill and the others were not, of course, radical in the contemporary sense. They were classical liberals who defended property

[1] Michael St. John Packe, *The Life of John Stuart Mill* (New York: Martin Secker & Warburg Ltd, 1954), 454.

[2] This sketch is drawn principally from Mill's autobiography, John Stuart Mill, "*Autobiography*," in *Autobiography and Literary Essays* as part of *Collected Works of John Stuart Mill (CW)*, ed. John M. Robson (Toronto: University of Toronto Press, 1978), vol. 1:1–290 and from the following sources: Alexander Bain, *John Stuart Mill: A Criticism with Personal Recollections* (London: Longman & Company, 1882); Michael St. John Packe, *The Life of John Stuart Mill* (New York: Capricorn Books, 1970); Nicholas Capaldi, *John Stuart Mill: A Biography* (Cambridge: Cambridge University Press, 2004); F. A. Hayek, *John Stuart Mill and Harriet Taylor: Their Friendship and Subsequent Marriage* (New York: A. M. Kelley, 1951); Alan Ryan, *J. S. Mill* (London: Routledge & Kegan Paul, 1974).

rights, free markets and a broadened democratic franchise. But their views evolved from very different premises than the classical liberals of the previous century – John Locke and Adam Smith, in particular. They were thoroughly secular in their outlook, rejecting Locke's Christianity and Smith's deism. They grounded the case for liberty not on natural rights or social contract ideas, which predominated in the seventeenth and eighteenth centuries, or later Smith's "invisible hand" theory, with its lingering intimation of a benevolent Providence. Instead, they believed it was human happiness – the utilitarian principle of "the greatest happiness of the greatest number" – which should govern social and political reform.

James Mill, had decided to make of his son an archetype of enlightened intellectuality – a utilitarian, a reformer and, as the elder Mill wrote to Bentham, "a successor worthy of us."[3] Today we would say that his father home-schooled Mill with a vengeance. The elder Mill was of Scottish Presbyterian stock and, though he rejected early in life the substance of that religion, he retained to the end the highly disciplined emotional austerity of his Calvinist forebears. Mill described his father as utterly dispassionate, rational, a Stoic. He tells us that James Mill regarded the expression of every passionate emotion "a form of madness." He regarded human life as "a poor thing at best" and often said that he "never knew a happy old man."[4]

In the first draft of his autobiography, Mill wrote candidly of his father's "baneful" influence on the emotional lives of his children. "My father's children neither loved him with any warmth of affection," Mill remembered, "nor [did] anyone else." In a later draft he toned this down, saying simply that while he did not love his father, he was always devoted to him.[5] His comments about his mother are even less flattering, if that is possible. She was the beautiful and vivacious daughter of a wealthy widow when James Mill married her, but she was uneducated. Though she bore him nine children, he seems to have regarded her with chilly contempt. Mill himself thought her a shallow drudge who was guilty by omission of curing his father's, or her children's, emotional distance.

> That rarity in England, a really warm-hearted mother, would … have made my father a totally different being and … would have made the children loving and being loved. But my mother, with the very best intentions, only knew how to pass her life in drudging for them. Whatever she could do for them, she did, and they liked her because she was kind to them, but to make herself loved, looked up to or even obeyed, required qualities which she unfortunately did not possess.[6]

[3] Jeremy Bentham, *The Works of Jeremy Bentham*, ed. John Bowring (Edinburgh: William Tait, 1838–43), 10:473, which is cited in a separately published autobiography of Mill. John Stuart Mill, *Autobiography* (Jack Stillinger, ed., 1969), xi.

[4] Mill, *Autobiography*, CW, 1:49, 51.

[5] Ibid., 1:53.

[6] Ibid., 612.

Mill tells us that his father shielded him from the association of other children so that they could get on with the business of his education. And so they did. He began to read ancient Greek at the age of three, beginning with Aesop's fables. He read Xenophon, Herodotus and some of Plato's dialogues – again, in the original Greek – by the age of seven. He also began reading broadly in history and commenced learning algebra, geometry and Latin by eight. At this point, Mill's father appointed him schoolmaster to his younger siblings. As the oldest of nine, Mill took the brunt of his father's pedagogical zeal. A slip in the Latin lesson and he would be sent to bed without dinner. Everything he argued or wrote was torn up and thrown back to him to refine and perfect. As he wrote in his autobiography, "I grew up in the absence of love and in the presence of fear."[7]

With or without love, Mill's education continued at an almost unbelievable pace. By ten, he could read Plato's dialogues fluently in the original Greek and at twelve; he began the study of logic and political economy. A year later he was busy preparing paragraph summaries of his father's *Elements of Political Economy* which was used as a text in British universities for several decades. When Mill was fourteen, he spent a year in France as a guest of Bentham's brother, Sir Samuel Bentham. There he learned French, read French literature, hiked in the Pyrenees and took university-level classes in logic, philosophy of science and chemistry, among others. He met the economist, Jean-Baptiste Say and saw Saint-Simon, whose socialism and progressive conception of history would later influence him. This period set the stage for his lifelong love of the French who, in contrast to the English, did not find in every other individual "an enemy or a bore."[8]

Mill's education was broad and "liberal," in the classical sense, but accomplished under the auspices of a stern secularism.[9] James Mill had studied Divinity at Edinburgh University and was licensed as a pastor upon graduation, but soon lost his faith. He held Butler's *Analogy* in high regard, though for exactly the opposite reason intended by its author. Where Butler defended orthodox Christianity from deism by showing that every argument deists leveled against Christianity could be leveled against deism itself, the elder Mill accepted the thrust of Butler's argument but broadened its target – rejecting both Christianity and deism together. Mill called his father a modern-day Lucretius – a materialist and an agnostic who imparted these instincts to his son:

> It would have been wholly inconsistent with my father's ideas of duty, to allow me to acquire impressions contrary to his convictions and feelings respecting religion: and he impressed upon me from the first that the manner in which the world came

7 Ibid. Or as a recent commentator put it, "Mill's education was 'the most liberal and the least liberal education possible. The world's greatest liberal was indoctrinated with liberalism.'" Stephen Priest, *The British Empiricists* (London: Penguin Books, 1990), 174.

8 Mill, *Autobiography*, CW, 1:61.

9 Ibid., 41–43 (discussing Mill's agnosticism).

> into existence was a subject on which nothing was known: that the question "Who made me?" cannot be answered because we have no experience or authentic information from which to answer it.... I am one of those very few examples in this country of one who has not thrown off religious belief, but never had it. I looked upon the modern exactly as I had the ancient religion as something which in no way concerned me.[10]

Mill's attitude toward the spiritual was complex. Although he was dismissive of orthodox Christianity, he was not a true atheist. He resisted reductive forms of materialism and, by the end of his life, came around to the view that, if a supremely good God existed, which he thought possible, He could not be all-powerful. There was simply too much pain and evil in the world for God to be both perfectly good and omnipotent.

When Mill was fifteen, he was finally permitted to read Bentham – an event which produced in him a reaction far more than philosophical. The "greatest happiness principle," a term Bentham had borrowed from Joseph Priestley, promised a new kind of morality. Indeed, it promised a new kind of world – one in which the ultimate touchstone of "good" and "bad" could be reduced to collective human happiness which, for Bentham, was nothing other than the totality of the pleasurable sensations that might be had by all sentient creatures. Mill's existence now assumed a kind of quasi-spiritual quest that encompassed all humanity. He decided immediately upon reading Bentham that the goal of his life was to be "a reformer of the world."[11]

The pace of his youthful career only picked up from this point. Between the ages of sixteen and nineteen, he founded a debating club, which he named "the Utilitarian Society." (He later claimed to be the first to use the term "utilitarian" in its philosophical sense.[12]) Even his youthful anti-authoritarianism was appropriately directed toward good, progressive causes. Though it was hushed up at the time, it came out at the end of Mill's life that he had spent a night in jail at the age of sixteen for distributing birth control literature in the East End.[13]

He also became a regular contributor to the *Westminster Review*, a Benthamite journal of political and social criticism, and for about eighteen months became Bentham's personal secretary and editor. Among other tasks, it was the young Mill's job to gather, collate and massage into coherent essays a multitude of scraps of paper with thoughts and references, which Bentham customarily pinned to the curtain behind his desk. His education, Mill later said, gave him a quarter-century head start on his peers – and then took its toll.

At twenty, Mill suffered what can only be described as a nervous breakdown. The event was precipitated by a simple question he posed to himself one day:

[10] Ibid., 45.
[11] Ibid., 137.
[12] John Stuart Mill, "Utilitarianism," in *Essays on Ethics, Religion and Society*, *CW*, 10:209, n.
[13] Packe, *Life of Mill*, 57–58.

> "Suppose that all your objects in life were realized; that all the changes in institutions and opinions which you are looking forward to could be realized at this very instant: would this be a great joy and happiness to you?" And an irrepressible self-consciousness distinctly answered "no." At this, my heart sank within me; the whole foundation on which my life was constructed fell down. ... I seemed to have nothing left to live for.[14]

He spent the next six months in a semi-dissociated haze, robotically going through his day-to-day routine with little sense of commitment, let alone enjoyment. He concluded that the "habit of analysis," which his father had so carefully cultivated in him had "a tendency to wear away the feelings." His capacity for stripping everything down and analyzing it into a virtual nothingness left him with a "perpetual worm at the root both of the passions and the virtues."[15] Mill's profound sense of psychological dislocation only deepened when a friend pointed out that others viewed Mill as a "made man" (i.e., a manufactured personality).[16] Both his recovery and his very sense of self-identity required a radical act of self-assertion – an act, characteristically, which could only unfold for him on the plane of ideas.

ROMANTICISM AND MILL'S "TRANSITION"

It was in the fall of 1828, still laboring under the lingering effects of his "mental crisis" when Mill, now twenty-two, discovered the poetry of the romantics. At first, he read Byron but, predictably, this only deepened his depression. The bucolic simplicity of Wordsworth, on the other hand, lifted him from his malaise, producing in him a joyful coterie of "sympathetic and imaginative pleasures" detached from all worldly strife. The "Intimations of Immortality" was one of his favorites. Even when the tone was melancholy, no one but Wordsworth could express with such sonorous sweetness Mill's own yearning for a lost innocence:

> THERE was a time when meadow, grove, and stream,
> The earth, and every common sight,
> To me did seem
> Apparell'd in celestial light,
> The glory and the freshness of a dream.
> It is not now as it hath been at yore;—
> Turn wheresoe'er I may,
> By night or day,
> The things which I have seen I now can see no more.

[14] Mill, *Autobiography*, CW, 1:139.
[15] Ibid., 141.
[16] Ibid., 163.

Mill followed his discovery of Wordsworth with the poetry and philosophy of Coleridge, the symphonies of Weber and the "anti-self-consciousness theory of Carlyle" – all influences which served to counterbalance the old "habit of analysis."

Romanticism, in sum, offered Mill a spiritual respite from his father's and Bentham's arid utilitarianism. Whereas utilitarianism was utterly rational, collectivistic and reductionist, romanticism was an eclectic and expansive philosophy. The romantics exalted nature over convention, originality over tradition, imagination over reason and the aesthetic over the ethical. They valued authentic emotions and placed the highest value on individuality. Often intermingled with the idealism of such thinkers as Kant, Fichte and Hegel, it represented for nineteenth-century intellectuals a middle way between traditional Christianity and what many regarded as the barren rationalism of eighteenth-century philosophy. It was a surrogate for religion, a spiritual salve for an increasingly skeptical society. In lieu of God, it offered Spirit; in place of the immortal soul, the authentic self. If there is truth to be found in life, it was not to be had in the brute facticity of the external world and certainly not in the commands of some distant lawgiver. Rather, truth could only be realized in the recesses of the individual self and, in particular, in the life of the authentic genius who lives passionately according to his own plan of existence.

Mill was far too analytical a thinker to accept much of the philosophical substance of romanticism, but the romantic *spirit* rekindled his joy for life. He began to sense what he called the "many-sidedness" of truth (a term he used again in his defense of freedom of expression). Yes, there was truth in utilitarianism, but in light of his nervous breakdown, he began to suspect that happiness could not be so straightforwardly pursued. "Ask yourself whether you are happy," he wrote in the Autobiography, "and you cease to be so. The only chance is to treat, not happiness, but some end external to it, as the purpose of life."[17] In fact, the pursuit of happiness might be considerably more circuitous than the utilitarians had suspected since a life of pleasure without struggle might cease to be pleasurable altogether.[18] Utilitarianism might tell us what to aim for, but we cannot aim for it directly. And even if the metaphysics of romanticism was a hopeless jumble, its quest for individual authenticity and self-development became the central animating principle of Mill's political and social thought.

Romanticism and idealism led Mill more deeply into the waters of Continental political thought. He began reading the French socialists, St. Simon, Auguste Comte and Pierre-Josef Proudhon, who famously declared, "property is theft." These influences obviously crashed against his father's and Bentham's classical

[17] Ibid., 147.

[18] "I felt that the flaw in my life," Mill wrote, "must be a flaw in life itself; that the question was, whether, if the reformers of society and government could succeed in their objects, and every person in the community were free and in a state of physical comfort, the pleasures of life, being no longer kept up by struggle and privation, would cease to be pleasures." Ibid., 149.

liberal commitments to free markets and property rights. But Mill found bits of truth on all sides. He began to be wary of any kind of dogmatism. At one point, he fancied himself a "mystic" but his friend, writer and philosopher, Thomas Carlyle, ten years Mill's senior, knew him better than Mill knew himself. He assured Mill that he was no mystic. On reflection, Mill agreed but suggested in response that perhaps his mission in life was "to translate the mysticism of others into the language of argument."[19]

This period in his twenties, which Mill referred to as his "transition," involved a conscious act of self-creation, a self-remaking of the "made man." He tells us that he meticulously evaluated every new influence – every new pattern of thought – turning it round in his mind, massaging those pieces that passed the test into the evolving firmament of what he wished to preserve from the past, modifying or discarding the rest.[20] He later reduced his experience in an essay written in 1832 "On Genius," in which he argued that genius was not limited to the artist or the discoverer of great truths: it is available to anyone who is willing to rethink for themselves the truths previously discovered by others.[21] This was a process of intellectual and, ultimately, *moral* self-transformation – a process that would later figure prominently in Mill's conception of liberty.

"THE MOST VALUABLE FRIENDSHIP OF MY LIFE"

If his nervous breakdown and subsequent intellectual transition was the first important defining event in his life, then meeting Harriet Taylor was the second. Mill was twenty-four and Taylor a year younger when they met. Mill was shy, sensitive, analytical and physically awkward (he had trouble even tying his shoes as a youth). Harriet was, by all accounts, a remarkable woman – vivacious, poetic and intuitive, a willowy beauty with deep-set eyes and a fiery wit. In turns, she was graceful and fierce, intense and kind – Carlyle called her "a living romantic heroine." Unfortunately for both, however, she was also married, the mother of two with a third child soon on the way. Her husband, John Taylor, was an amiable and prosperous wholesale druggist eleven years her senior. He was easy-going and of good liberal opinions – but she grew bored with him.

19 John Stuart Mill, "The Letters, 1812–1837," in *The Earlier Letters of John Stuart Mill 1812–1848*, CW, 12:219, Mill to Carlyle (March 2, 1834).

20 "I never, in the course of my transition, was content to remain, for ever so short a time, confused and unsettled. When I had taken in any new idea, I could not rest till I had adjusted its relation to my old opinions and ascertained exactly how far its effect ought to extend in modifying or superseding them." Mill, *Autobiography*, CW, 1:163, 165.

21 John Stuart Mill, "On Genius," in *Autobiography and Literary Essays*, CW, 1:327.

Harriet seems to have imagined herself a romantic idealist whose prospects had been corseted by the fetters of married life. She and Mill met through the Unitarian preacher, W. J. Fox, who was popular among London's fashionably liberal intelligentsia. Fox had become the legal guardian of two teenage sisters, Eliza and Sally Flowers. Though Fox was married, he soon commenced a scandalous relationship with Eliza, whom Mill may have at first fancied. Perhaps in an effort to put Mill off the track, Fox introduced him to Eliza's closest friend, Harriet, with whom Mill was soon smitten. Carlyle characteristically described Fox's bohemian circle as "a flight of really wretched-looking 'friends of the species.'"[22]

If the details of Mill's and Harriet's arrangement seem bizarre by contemporary standards, they scandalized Victorian London of the early 1830s. Mill was at first certain that Harriet would sue for divorce. The two had even considered running off to Australia. Mr. Taylor was convinced that Harriet would eventually repent the relationship. He sent her to Paris with the children for a six-month cooling-off period, but Mill followed her there. It soon became clear that Harriet had her own compromise in mind: she could only remain loyal to each man by renouncing sexual relations with both. Harriet wrote to Mill, "Yes – these circumstances *do* require greater strength than any other – the greatest – that which you have & which if you had not I should never have loved you."[23] Mill reluctantly obliged, as did her husband after some feeble protests. The Taylors' marriage continued on these chilly terms for the next twenty years. Harriet managed their house and raised their children, but accompanied Mill publicly to concerts and lectures and vacationed with him in Europe. Mill was even permitted to dine with her two nights a week at her residence while John Taylor supped at his club.[24]

During this period, Mill terminated one friendship after another at even the gentlest suggestion that he and Harriet treat their public relationship with a modicum of discretion.[25] When James Mill pressed his son about the affair, Mill responded that he had no other feelings about Harriet than he would have toward an equally

[22] In a letter to his father, Carlyle wrote, "They "struggle not in favor of duty being *done* but against duty of any kind being required. ... Most of these people are very indignant at marriage and the like, and frequently indeed, are obliged to divorce their own wives, or be divorced; for although this world is already blooming (or is one day to do it) in everlasting 'happiness of the greatest number, these peoples' own *houses* (I always find) are little hells of improvidence, discord and unreason." Carlyle initially exempted Mill from this criticism even though Mill soon began to be seen publicly with the married Mrs. Taylor. Thomas Carlyle to Dr. John Carlyle (July 28, 1834), excerpted in Hayek, *John Stuart Mill and Harriet Taylor*, 82.

[23] Ibid., 60.

[24] Capaldi, *Mill: A Biography*, 107–8.

[25] Mill's icy treatment of his childhood friend, John Roebuck, was particularly harsh. Capaldi, *Mill: A Biography*, 111; Packe, *Life of Mill*, 152–53. But his treatment of his mother was even worse. As Alan Ryan put it, his mother "was distressed and bewildered by the violence with which her favorite son turned on her." Mill "was so completely in the wrong that it is painful to read the correspondence..." Ryan, *J. S. Mill*, 12.

able man. After his father died when Mill was 28, he would not permit his family, with whom he still lived, even to speak about Harriet in his presence. Mill's self-centeredness concerning their relationship is genuinely remarkable. Rather than recognizing the pain he must have caused Taylor, he complained in a letter to Carlyle that he was too self-critical for his own good: "I will and must … master it, or surely it will master me."[26] It is ironic that one of the most influential moral philosophers of the modern era could dismiss as a bout of excessive self-analysis what most anyone else would have suspected as the sting of conscience.

That said, there is general consensus among Mill's biographers that his and Harriet's twenty-year relationship before marriage remained chaste, and that it may have remained so even after marriage.[27] Mill's autobiography leaves only the vaguest suggestion otherwise.[28] Mill's friend, Alexander Bain, who had helped edit his *System of Logic*, insinuated that Mill simply had a weak libido.[29] An alternative explanation is that Mill and Harriet entertained a genuinely gnostic view of sex. Their early letters to each other resonate with the idea that intellectual liberation requires physical renunciation. "[G]ratification of the passion in the highest form," Mill wrote in one note, requires "restraining it in the lowest." They condemned bourgeois marriage, along with any restrictions on divorce, as an invention of the "sexualists." If only marriage "had as its goal the true happiness and development of both individuals, rather than their lower physical gratification," Mill wrote, "there would never have been any reason why law or opinion should have set any limits to the most unbounded freedom of uniting and separating."[30] Mill declared in a pointed diary entry from 1854, "I am anxious to leave on record at least in this place my deliberate opinion that any great improvement in human life is not to be looked for so long as the animal instinct of sex occupies the absurdly disproportionate place it [now] does."[31] So, it may well be that Mill remained celibate for his entire life.

Mill wrote these words three years into his marriage. He and Harriet had been married on Easter Monday, 1851, two years after John Taylor died. They were now in their mid-forties. Their friendship had endured for twenty years though the two had by now largely withdrawn from social engagements. Characteristically, Mill

[26] Capaldi, *Mill: A Biography*, 107.

[27] "It seems likely," Ryan observes, "that [Harriet] did not care for the sexual intimacies of married life, and was happier with the role of 'Seelenfreundin,' than that of middle-class wife." Ryan, *J. S. Mill*, 49; author note: *seelenfreundin*, rough translation *soul mate*.

[28] He wrote that, after years of a "partnership of thought, feeling and writing" marriage brought them into "a partnership of our entire existence." Mill, *Autobiography*, 1:247.

[29] Bain, *Mill: A Criticism with Personal Recollections*; Capaldi, *Mill: A Biography*, 380, n. 90.

[30] Hayek, *John Stuart Mill and Harriet Taylor*, 68.

[31] John Stuart Mill, "Diary, 1854," in *Journals and Debating Speeches Part II (1827)*, CW, 27:664 (entry of March 26, 1854).

used the occasion of their marriage to pen a formal letter of protest denouncing the "odious powers" the law gave husbands over wives and declared "that I absolutely disclaim and repudiate all pretensions to have acquired any rights whatever" over the woman he would marry.[32]

Mill's relations with his family only deteriorated after the marriage.

The fault was almost wholly Mill's. He had not invited either his mother or his remaining siblings to the ceremony; most were informed of the event by others after it took place. Worse, he rebuffed their subsequent attempts to smooth things over. Two of his sisters, Clara and Mary, tried to visit Mill and Harriet at their new home in Blackheath Park, deliberately chosen for its obscure location outside London. Mill refused to see them. A volley of letters followed from the sisters, written more from hurt than from disapprobation. He brushed each of them off in turn as "impertinent," "vulgar" and "insolent."

Mill's brother George, twenty years Mill's junior, wrote to Mill from shock and hurt, after hearing of the marriage. George was by now dying of tuberculosis in Madeira. Mill cut him off in a series of stiff letters. George committed suicide about a year later. Mill's mother attempted to visit him at the East India House, where he worked, but he had her turned away. More than two years later, as she was dying of liver cancer, she wrote again in the kindest of terms – "your Marriage gave us all pleasure as you had chosen a Wife who was capable of entering into all your pursuits and appreciate your good qualities..." Mill visited her only once during her final illness and went abroad for an extended vacation before she died. In his last letter to her, he asked to be relieved as executor of her will.[33]

Mill's and Harriet's marriage lasted only seven and a half years. Both suffered throughout from the tuberculosis which ultimately took their lives. Mill called it his "family disease" as it had already taken his father and several siblings. In fact, it is quite possible that Mill infected Harriet, as he suffered from the condition long before she did. But in her case, it developed much more quickly and took its ultimate toll while the two were travelling in Avignon, France, in November 1858. Mill wrote a frenzied letter from the Hotel d'Europe, where they were staying, to a doctor in Nice, offering one thousand pounds if he would come immediately, but Harriet succumbed before he arrived.

Scholars and commentators have speculated endlessly about the nature of Mill's and Harriet's relationship and her relative influence upon his work. Mill's exaggerations of Harriet's qualities and influence upon him are notorious: "Her mind... was a perfect instrument, piercing to the heart and marrow of the matter.... To be admitted into any degree of mental intercourse with a being of these qualities could not but have a most beneficial influence on my development....

32 Packe, *Life of Mill*, 348.
33 Ibid., 351–57.

The benefit I received was far greater than any which I could hope to give.... What I owe, even intellectually, to her is, almost infinite.... I have acquired more from her teaching than from all other sources taken together.... Were I but capable of interpreting to the world one half the great thoughts and noble feelings which are buried in her grave, I should be the medium of a greater benefit to it, than is every likely to arise from anything that I can write, unprompted and unassisted by her all but unrivaled wisdom."[34]

Perhaps these were the over-idealized expressions of a highly sublimated love, deepened by his profound grief at her loss. Harriet certainly had not had Mill's education and background. While she was well-read – particularly in literature, poetry and the philosophy of the romantic and socialist writers – her understanding of philosophy was limited and what she knew of economics she learned from Mill. Her forte, in general, was not primarily analytic.

Yet we should not underestimate Harriet's influence on Mill either – an influence both intellectual and emotional. As a young woman, she had written essays which anticipate some of the themes of *On Liberty* and the *Subjection of Women*.[35] Line by line she edited with him *On Liberty* and his *Autobiography*. She insisted that Mill include in the second edition of the *Principles of Political Economy* a chapter on "the Probable Future of the Labouring Classes" – a chapter which Mill later thought made the book most distinctive and which scholars think lends the book a socialistic cast. Over the course of their life together, Harriet pulled Mill in the direction of more radical causes, of socialism and of more fully libertarian views of the right to marry and divorce.[36] She drew out in him a more visceral sense of the plight of the downtrodden and the weak, and she helped him transform relatively abstract observations about the role of social institutions on gender into an impassioned feminism. Yet the most palpable of her influences may be found in the pages of *On Liberty* which Mill insisted was more their joint project than any of his other works.[37] Not only is this his greatest and most remembered book, it sparkles with the most vividly evocative and concretely powerful prose of all his works. If this alone were her influence, it would be substantial.

[34] Mill, *Autobiography*, CW, 1:195, 197. Harriet had actually toned down many of Mill's original comments in an earlier draft of the Autobiography which provided, as Ryan notes "an account of her talents which nobody but her second husband has ever thought remotely credible." Ryan, *J. S. Mill*, 14–15.

[35] Ibid., 125–27; see also Jo Ellen Jacobs, *The Voice of Harriet Taylor Mill* (Bloomington: Indiana University Press, 2002), 195–251 (for a sympathetic account of Harriet's intellectual and moral influence on Mill).

[36] As Mill admitted, were it not for Harriet, he "might have become a less thorough radical and democrat than I am." Mill, *Autobiography*, CW, 1:259.

[37] Ibid., 257.

MILL'S PRIVATE SIDE

Mill's relationship with Harriet, with his family and with those closest to him sheds fascinating light on Mill's character. Almost all who knew him describe him as a gentleman of the most refined moral sensibilities. Gladstone called him "the saint of rationalism." Yet, in the sphere that was perhaps his most underdeveloped, his romantic experiences, he could be genuinely self-centered to all but the object of his love, Harriet, to whom he remained uxoriously attached.

In other matters, Mill was scrupulously honest, assiduously principled and remarkably courageous. While running for Parliament, he was confronted with a comment he had made in one of his writings that most people in the working class were liars. When asked if he had written this by a gathering of working class voters, he responded, "I did." The crowd erupted in applause, apparently in appreciation for his candor.[38] While in office, he received almost weekly death threats, which he seems to have largely shrugged off.[39] He supported himself and Harriet on his own income after they married, refusing to take a penny from the substantial estate left by her late husband.[40]

Mill generously supported many friends and intellectuals who had fallen on hard times.[41] Herbert Spencer, the prophet of social Darwinism, had come to Mill's attention after he had attacked Mill's *System of Logic*. When Spencer found himself penniless, he came to Mill for assistance. Mill helped secure him a job at the East India Company and later supported him directly. More generally, he brought a combination of moral integrity and passion to bear in political and social matters where it was often most needed.

There were, to be sure, tensions in his worldview which affected his opinions of others. Though he was, theoretically, a democrat and an egalitarian, he exhibited an almost Brahministic aversion to contact with the untouchables of the lower classes. The expressions he used to describe them – "the mass," the "uncultivated herd," "unintellectual society," those of "a very common order" – bear this out. This aversion was occasionally comingled with a messianic sense of duty reminiscent of Bentham:

> To a person of any but a very common order of thought and feeling, much society, unless he has personal objects to serve by it, must be supremely unattractive: and most people in the present day, of any really high class of intellect, make their contact with it so slight, and at such long intervals, as to be almost considered as retiring from it altogether. Those persons of any mental superiority who do otherwise are, almost without exception, greatly deteriorated by it. Not to mention loss

38 Ibid., 274.
39 Ibid., 282.
40 Capaldi, *Mill: A Biography*, 228–29 (Mill wrote a letter disavowing any right to her property).
41 Packe, *Life of Mill*, 484. For example, Mill long supported Herbert Spencer. Ibid., 453.

of time, the tone of their feelings is lowered.... A person of high intellect should never go into unintellectual society unless he can enter it as an apostle....[42]

Nor were strangers exempt from Mill's condescension. In a letter to Harriet, he smugly sized up a fellow Englishman, a man named Pope, whom Mill met while traveling in France in 1855:

> He turned out a pleasant person to meet, as, though he does not seem to me to have any talent, he is better informed than common Englishmen – knows a good deal of French history, for example, especially that of the Revolution – and seems to have already got to, or seems to be quite ready to receive, all our opinions. I tried him on religion, where I found him quite what we think right, on politics – on which he was somewhat more than a radical – on the equality of women which he seems not to have quite dared to think of himself but seemed to adopt it at once – and to be ready for all reasonable socialism – he boggled a little at limiting the power of bequest which I was glad of as it showed that the other agreements were not merely following a lead taken. He was therefore worth talking to and I think he will have taken away a great many ideas from me.[43]

The worst excesses are found in his heady private correspondence with Harriet. He frequently distinguished himself and Harriet from others in almost ontological terms:

> But will the morality which suits the highest natures, in this matter, be also best for all inferior natures? My conviction is that it will, but this can be only a happy accident. All of the difficulties of morality, in any of its brands, grow out of the conflict which continually arises between the highest morality & even the best popular morality which the degree of development achieved by average human nature, will allow to exist.[44]

These flourishes can perhaps be excused in light of their youth, Mill's utter dearth of romantic experience and the romantic cult of genius, which seem to have contributed to the hothouse spirit emblematic of some of their exchanges. Nevertheless, the claim by one of his most famous defenders that Mill was utterly without vanity cannot be entirely sustained.[45] A more objective assessment would be that, while Mill regularly downplayed his own considerable abilities – he once said that any average

[42] Mill, *Autobiography*, *CW*, 1:235. Bentham had referred to himself as "the Luther of jurisprudence." When Lord Shelburne asked Bentham what could be done to save the nation, Bentham answered, "take my book and follow me." John Lawrence Hill, *After the Natural Law* (San Francisco: Ignatius Press, 2016), 218.

[43] Packe, *Life of Mill*, 373.

[44] Hayek, *John Stuart Mill and Harriet Taylor*, 60.

[45] Isaiah Berlin, who wrote extensively on Mill, described him as "clear-headed, candid, highly articulate, intensely serious, and without any trace of fear, vanity or humor." Isaiah Berlin, "John Stuart Mill and the Ends of Life," *Four Essays on Liberty* (Oxford: Oxford University Press, 1969), 177. But Alan Ryan's description – that Mill possessed "an extraordinary combination of arrogance and self-deprecation" – appears more apt. Ryan, *J. S. Mill*, 127.

boy or girl could have done what he did given the same education – he frequently offered scathing reviews of lesser minds with whom he disagreed. Conservatives were "the stupid party." Any politician who did not see the value of his theory of voting "may be pronounced an incompetent statesman, unequal to the politics of the future."[46] Dr. Whewell's book, *Elements of Morality*, an intuitionist philosophy that clashed with Mill's empiricism, was "one of the thousand waves on the dead sea of commonplace."[47]

Yet Mill could be charming and downright funny and frequently achieved some of his most devastating results with more than a modicum of wit. While in Parliament, another member confronted him with his comment about "the stupid party." Mill responded:

> I never meant to say that the Conservatives are generally stupid. I meant to say that stupid people are generally Conservative. I believe that this is so obviously and universally admitted a principle that I hardly think any gentleman will deny it. Suppose any party, in addition to the share it may possess of the ability of the community, has nearly the whole of its stupidity, that party must, by the law of its constitution, be the stupidest party: and I do not see at all why honourable gentlemen should see that position as at all offensive to them, for it ensures their being always an extremely powerful party.... There is so much dense, solid force in sheer stupidity that anybody of able men with that force pressing behind them may ensure victory in many a struggle, and many a victory the Conservative party has gained through that power.[48]

There was a pause as the other members took this in and then – the entire chamber went up in a roar of laughter.

Similarly, when he learned that Carlyle had addressed a public banquet in Edinburgh, joining in a drinking song lampooning Mill's philosophy that ended with the refrain

> Stuart Mill on Mind and Matter,
> Stuart Mill on Mind and Matter,
> Stuart Mill exerts his skill
> To make an end of Mind and Matter,

Mill wrote to Carlyle, "Please thank Mrs. Carlyle for her remembrance of me. I have been sorry to hear a rather poor account of her health, and to see by your Edinburgh address that your own is not quite satisfactory."[49]

[46] Mill, *Autobiography*, *CW*, 1:262.
[47] Packe, *Life of Mill*, 255.
[48] Ibid., 454.
[49] Ibid., 445–46.

MILL'S PUBLISHED WORKS, MEMBER OF PARLIAMENT AND FINAL YEARS

Mill never attended university. As a free-thinker, he refused to sign on to the Thirty-Nine articles required for admission to Oxford or Cambridge in the 1820s. (Bentham had signed this and regretted doing so for the rest of his life.) Instead, Mill attended some lectures by John Austin, among others, at University College, London – the university Bentham later helped found for free-thinkers, Catholics and Jews. Of course, even by the time he would have attended university, Mill's education had already far surpassed that of other university students. Thus, rather than taking time out to continue his education, he commenced his professional career in 1823, aged seventeen, at the British East India Company. He remained there for the rest of his professional life.

The corpus of Mill's *Collected Works* – including his books, essays, letters and speeches – spans thirty-two corpulent volumes. His assiduous work ethic was well-known, his output prodigious, especially considering that he had essentially worked full-time until the age of 52. During his thirty-five years of employment, he frequently worked from 8 in the morning until early or mid-afternoon, and then would begin his more intellectual work, reading, writing and corresponding with thinkers and statesman from all over Europe and America.

His first important publication was *A System of Logic*. Of all his works, it remains his most philosophically ambitious and wide-ranging – an audacious, encyclopedic six-volume treatise covering the disciplines of logic, mathematics, the physical sciences, psychology, sociology, politics and moral theory. It took him thirteen years to write and was finally published in 1843, when he was thirty-seven. Mill's grand goal in the "Logic" was nothing less than to unite, on one positivistic foundation, the hard and soft sciences, moral theory, and social and political thought. It was, in essence, the philosophical foundation for all of his later political work. In this work, we can see that he had begun to lay the groundwork for his political vision well before *On Liberty*.

Because of the length and depth of the multivolume treatise, Mill anticipated that the *Logic* would not be a popular work. Yet the book began to appear in bookstores and was quickly adopted as the canonical text on philosophy of science at Oxford and then Cambridge. Glowing reviews appeared in the *Westminster Review* and other places, but the review that delighted him most was a one-hundred-page attack on the *Logic* which appeared in the conservative journal, the *British Critic*. It declared that, if this work "be adopted as a full statement of the truth, the whole fabric of Christian theology must totter and fall."[50]

The *Principles of Political Economy* followed five years later, in 1848. It was the most advanced work of economic theory to date, and applied the principles he developed in the *System of Logic* to the sphere of economics. Here Mill advanced a kind

[50] Ibid., 272.

of *modus vivendi* between the laissez-faire theories of earlier classical liberals and the more aggressive forms of socialism and communism which began to be popularized in the 1830s and 1840s. He had been influenced by the French socialists – Fourier, Saint-Simon and Comte – in important ways and called himself an "ideal socialist." He went so far as to claim that, if the choice were between Communism and economic arrangements as they then existed in the 1840s, "all of the difficulties, great or small, of Communism, would be but dust in the balance." Yet these were not the only two choices: laissez-faire, property rights and economic prosperity could be perfected if properly qualified and directed toward the right end – personal autonomy.

Mill's social and political ideal was a decentralized, meritocratic society of truly autonomous entrepreneurs who owned or managed businesses and shared in the profits. The chief end of economics is not wealth maximization or equality of distribution; it is the promotion of self-development, individuality and autonomy. Accordingly, he consistently opposed most government regulation of the economy and even anticipated the Hayekian critique that economic centralization was rationally impossible. Yet he also disliked the wage system – a hangover, he thought, of feudalism. Mill hated aristocracy and its economic vestiges. He argued for the (compensated) liquidation of large, landed estates and for the abolition of entail and primogeniture, practices which prevented the subdivision, through inheritance, of large estates.

The *Principles* went through thirty-two editions in Mill's lifetime alone and became the standard textbook in economics in British universities into the early twentieth century.

Together, the *System of Logic* and the *Principles of Political Economy* sealed Mill's fame and galvanized his intellectual authority. By the 1850s, when he was in his early forties, he was recognized as the most important public intellectual in England. Lord Balfour, who was no acolyte of Mill's (he would later become a Conservative Prime Minister) recalled that Mill's authority at this time rivaled Hegel's in Germany a quarter century earlier. Leslie Stephens said that at Cambridge, during the 1850s and '60s, the answer to every question was "read Mill."[51]

Three years after the publication of the *Principles*, Mill and Harriet were married, in April 1851. For the next seven years, they largely withdrew from society. Mill published no substantial works during this time. Yet, even then, he was working on the next series of books – books that would seal his fame not with his own generation, as had his earlier work, but with posterity. He began writing *Utilitarianism* and *On Liberty* – the latter with Harriet's assistance – in 1854.

In 1856, Mill was promoted to Examiner of Indian Correspondence, a position which has been compared to that of India's Secretary of State. When, two years later,

[51] Gertrude Himmelfarb, "Editor's Introduction" to the Penguin edition of *On Liberty* (Harmondsworth: Penguin, 1974).

the British government proposed dissolving the company in favor of direct colonial administration by the Crown, Mill was tasked with drafting a major memorandum defending the company and, by implication, British imperialism. This required him to take a position that many have charged conflicts with his liberalism. He defended British rule in India (and in China) on grounds that these once-great nations had now fallen into barbarism. It was the duty of Britain to administer these colonies until such time as they could govern themselves.[52] When the government proceeded with dissolution of the company anyway, Mill was offered – and declined – an advisory role in the new administration. He retired in October 1858, to take an extended trip to France with Harriet – the trip that would turn out to be their last. Within a month of Mill's retirement, Harriet was gone.

After Harriet's death in November 1858 came the outpouring of his greatest books on which he had been working for the last several years – *On Liberty* in early 1859, *Considerations on Representative Government* in 1861 and *Utilitarianism*, which appeared in supplements to *Fraser's Magazine*, in 1861 and was published in book form a year later. He returned to pure philosophy with the publication of the ponderous *An Examination of Sir William Hamilton's Philosophy* in 1865. He had two reasons for writing this book. The first was straightforwardly philosophical. Hamilton, who had died in 1856, was perhaps the most important Scottish philosopher of the nineteenth century and was highly influential in the universities. His philosophy, sometimes referred to as "intuitionism," was a fusion of the Scottish "common sense" philosophy of Thomas Reid and the German idealism of Kant. Somewhat crudely put, intuitionists were given to the notion that we simply "know" certain things – that God exists, that certain acts are right or wrong – by a direct act of intuition. This clashed with Mill's inductive empiricism and led to substantive positions that were at odds with Mill's own philosophical conclusions.

The *Examination* was thus, on one level, a development of some of the more important themes from a *System of Logic*. He again wrestled with many of the chestnuts of traditional philosophy – the nature of the mind and the self, free will and determinism, and the existence of God. In the most memorable line of the book, while reflecting on the "problem of evil" – the apparent inconsistency of the existence of so much pain and evil in the world with an all-loving, all-powerful God – Mill observed:

> Whatever power such a being may have over me, there is one thing which he shall not do; he shall not compel me to worship him. I will call no being good who is not what I mean when I apply that epithet to my fellow creatures; and if such a creature can sentence me to hell for not so calling him, *to hell I will go*.[53]

[52] John Stuart Mill, "A Few Words on Non-Intervention," in *Essays on Equality, Law, and Education*, CW, 21:109–23.

[53] John Stuart Mill, "An Examination of Sir William Hamilton's Philosophy," in *An Examination of William Hamilton's Philosophy*, CW, 9:103 (my emphasis).

That same year, 1865, Mill published *Auguste Comte and Positivism* as a two-part article in the *Westminster Review*. This appeared in book form a year later. Mill had admired Comte as a younger man and had been deeply influenced by Comte's positivism, his socialism and his progressive idea of history. But with time, Comte's views had ossified into an oppressive totalitarian socialism. Comte proposed total state control of the economy and of all outlets of information, guided by a clerisy of enlightened intellectuals – something like a combination of the political philosophies of Plato and Chairman Mao. Comte's chauvinistic views of women only intensified Mill's contempt for his political views. Mill had Comte in mind when he declared in a letter to Harriet in 1855, announcing his intention to write a book on liberty, that "almost all the projects of the social reformers in these days are really liberticide – Comte."[54] In his *Autobiography*, he called Comte's political vision "the completest system of spiritual and temporal despotism which ever yet emanated from a human brain."[55] In sum, Mill wrote *Auguste Comte and Positivism* to rescue positivism from the clutches of scientism and totalitarianism.

In 1865, Mill reluctantly accepted calls for him to stand for election as M.P. for Westminster for the Liberal party. He refused to canvas, would not spend a penny on the campaign and answered all questions with complete candor, refusing to hide his more unpopular opinions. In general, he did everything he could to dissuade the voters – but won the election anyway.

He called himself an "advanced Liberal" and frequently dissented from his own party on important issues. In his first speech in Parliament, he opposed a proposal by a fellow Liberal to have the government subsidize losses by ranchers after a plague had wiped out the cattle population. Mill opposed such bailouts on principle, adding wryly that cattle owners had already been duly indemnified by the now-inflated price of meat. He later brooked a chorus of howls and laughter – even from among fellow Liberals – in advocating for female suffrage. And, opposing Liberals and Tories alike, he attacked a preemptive proposal to revoke Habeas Corpus in Ireland in response to an anticipated rebellion there.

Mill's utilitarianism occasionally led him to take stands favored by conservatives. He opposed a bill to abolish capital punishment on grounds that the death penalty is a deterrent to violent crime. He supported a Tory proposal to permit the interdiction by the British navy of neutral vessels carrying goods to countries which were enemies of Britain. Indeed, Mill was no pacifist. He decried the weakening of the British navy as "a national blunder" and argued for the abolition of the standing army and the creation of an Israeli-style citizen army in which all able-bodied men would serve for a period during their lives. A few years earlier, at the inception of the American Civil War, he wrote an impassioned piece

54 John Stuart Mill, *The Later Letters of John Stuart Mill*, CW, 14:294, Mill to Harriet (January 15, 1855).
55 Mill, *Autobiography*, CW, 1:221.

supporting the North – a position that was unpopular in Britain at the time. In opposition to those who decried war, he wrote:

> War is an ugly thing, but not the ugliest of things: the decayed and degraded state of moral and patriotic feeling which thinks nothing worth a war is worse. … A man who has nothing that he cares more about than he does his personal safety, is a miserable creature who has no chance of being free, unless made and kept so by the exertions of better men than himself.[56]

In sum, sticking to his own principles, Mill managed to infuriate all sides at one time or another during his three years in Parliament. He lost his seat when Parliament was disbanded after a cadre of more conservative liberals sided with the Tories, reacting against the Reform Bill which Mill supported. This bill, which doubled the number of eligible voters among the working class, soon became law anyway – cynically passed by Disraeli and the conservatives after they took control of Parliament. Indeed, within a few years, almost all of Mill's other highest priorities became law as well – land reforms in Ireland, the disestablishment of the Protestant Church there; the Married Women's Property Act, the National Education Act and the abolition of religious tests in the universities – the same tests which had kept him from studying at Oxford or Cambridge.

Privately, Mill was happy to leave Parliament and to reclaim his personal life. It was 1868. He was now 62. After retiring, he published his last important work, *The Subjection of Women*. He had written it in 1861 in the wake of Harriet's death but, because he knew it would be wildly unpopular, did not publish it until 1869. As he expected, conservatives and liberals alike denounced the book. Even some of his more forward-looking friends like Bain and Spencer distanced themselves from Mill's then-radical views on women. We will discuss *The Subjection of Women* at greater length in Chapter 7.

Mill also left a large, unfinished manuscript published after his death under the title of *Chapters on Socialism*, in which he advanced his arguments for a decentralized, autonomy-centered form of socialism. He praised the softer socialism of Fourier and Proudhon, opposed central planning and the nationalization of all property and forcefully distanced himself from Marxists and the revolutionary English workers' movements, which were, he charged, motivated more by "hate" than by the desire to improve the lot of the working class.

Mill's work on *Chapters on Socialism* indicate that he was moving increasingly in the direction of socialism toward the end of his life. Some have even suggested that, if he had lived, he would have eventually embraced Fabian socialism, but this latter claim is doubtful. Over the course of his life, Mill's socialism slowly overtook

[56] John Stuart Mill, "The Contest in America," in *Essays on Equality Law, and Education*, CW, 21:141–42.

several of his more libertarian tendencies, but he consistently resisted most forms of direct government intervention into the economy. And he remained concerned to the end that socialism would undercut what he regarded as the most vital human imperative – the need for self-reliance, autonomy and self-development. In sum, as we will see at greater length later, Mill never fully resolved the apparent conflict between his socialism and his libertarianism.

The picture of his last few years is poignant. Most of his time was spent at Avignon, among his books and effects, in the villa he had purchased a short walk from Harriet's grave. He had furnished it with the furniture from the room at the Hotel d'Europe in which she had died. His only and almost constant companion during these last years was Harriet's daughter, Helen Taylor, increasingly pugnacious and priggish with age – but always protective of Mill.

In 1872, a year before his death, Mill and Helen agreed to become godparents to the grandson of Lord John Russell who had served as Prime Minister while Mill was in Parliament. Russell's son and his wife, Lord and Lady Amberly, were a fairy-tale couple – young, rich, beautiful, aristocratic and very "advanced" in their political and social ideas. Mill kindled a close relationship with them and, though he had doubts about the term "godfather," agreed to take on this role with their young son.

Sadly, things ended tragically for the couple shortly after Mill's own death. Lady Amberly died of diphtheria in 1874, when the boy was two, and her husband, who never recovered from his grief, died a year later. Though Mill died before he could have any real influence on the child, the boy – Bertrand Russell – became one of the most important philosophers and social critics of the twentieth century. In striking ways, Russell's own philosophy – his skepticism of mind and matter, his liberalism and his decidedly anti-Christian sentiments – echoed Mill's own views.

Notwithstanding the "family illness," Mill remained in fairly robust health until the end of his life. He had kept his health up through the years by walking and frequently walked ten to twenty miles in a day. But on the Saturday before he died, he walked fifteen miles in the hot sun and came down with a fever a day later. He summoned from Nice the same doctor whom he had called to attend to Harriet. The doctor arrived – in time, on this occasion – but only to inform Mill that this latest attack would be fatal. Mill accepted the pronouncement with equanimity.

He died a few days later, on Wednesday, May 7, 1873, at 7:00 in the morning.[57] His last words, spoken to Helen Taylor, were characteristically, "You know that I have done my work."

He was interred with Harriet the following day, before most of his family and friends had even learned of his death.

57 Popular internet sources frequently report his death as May 8 but two reliable biographies agree that it was on the 7th. The cause of death was an erysipelas, a fever endemic to the region of southern France. Capaldi, *Mill: A Biography*, 356; Packe, *Life of Mill*, 507.

2

Liberalism before Mill

By the time Mill published *On Liberty* in 1859, liberalism in its "classical" form had existed for well more than a century. Scholars usually trace the origins of classical liberalism to John Locke's *Second Treatise of Government*, published anonymously in 1690, and such other works as his three *Letters on Toleration*. In the *Second Treatise*, Locke defended limited government, individual rights to life, liberty and property, religious toleration, a free market and popular sovereignty – themes that soon assumed a central role in the classical liberal tradition.

Nevertheless, the first writer to use the term "liberal" in its political and economic sense was probably Adam Smith, who wrote in *The Wealth of Nations* (published in 1776) that every man should "pursue his own interest his own way upon the liberal plan of equality, liberty and justice."[1] It was not until the 1820s, during Mill's youth, that the terms "liberal" and "conservative" began to be used in their modern senses. By the 1850s, Mill would use the term "advanced liberal" to describe himself and others who began to depart from the dogmas of classical liberalism and to embrace increasingly socialist and radical ideas.

The relatively recent use of the terms "liberal" and "conservative" means that the debates over the American Constitution, which took place in the late 1780s, did not unfold on liberal-versus-conservative lines. Indeed, it is difficult to place the Federalists and the Anti-federalists into either a modern "liberal" or "conservative" camp.[2] The Anti-federalists were small "d" democrats, agrarians, populists and "states-righters" who were opposed to concentrated executive and senatorial

[1] F. A. Hayek, *The Constitution of Liberty* (London: Routledge, 1960), 530, n. 13.

[2] Part of the reason for this, undoubtedly, is that the term "conservative" is itself usually used in the United States today as a designation for classical liberalism, while "liberal" refers to modern "progressive" liberalism. See John Lawrence Hill, *The Political Centrist* (Nashville: Vanderbilt University Press, 2009), 11–63 (discussing the origins and mutations of the terms "liberal" and "conservative" over the last two centuries).

power. They also tended to favor the inclusion of a bill of rights in the Constitution.[3] The Federalists favored a larger republic, free trade, Whiggish or classical liberal economic policies, and more centralization of power at the federal level. They were usually more skeptical about the inclusion of a bill of rights.[4] Only by looking back somewhat anachronistically can we see that Federalist John Adams was an early exemplar of American conservatism and Thomas Jefferson, father of the Democratic-Republican Party, was a beacon of liberalism.[5]

What is it that makes Locke the first genuinely "liberal" thinker? Of course, he favored policies that classical liberals came to endorse. But there is a deeper reason for viewing Locke as the father of the liberal tradition. Put simply, with Hobbes, he was the first to directly challenge the central assumption of all previous political thought going back to Plato and Aristotle. But, unlike Hobbes, he followed this with a recognizably "liberal" political prescription.

LOCKE'S CLASSICAL LIBERALISM

The defining attribute of classical political thought was the principle, as Aristotle declared in his *Politics*, that "the state is by nature prior to the family and the individual."[6] He did not mean that the individual was not important or, as fascist philosophers claimed in the twentieth century, that the individual exists for the benefit of the state. Aristotle was no collectivist. Rather, the purpose of the state – by which he meant all of our political and social institutions outside the household, for the Greeks did not yet distinguish between the political and the social – was to create the conditions necessary for the "good life" of the individual. There is a natural end – or telos – and the state's function is to help people achieve this.

What makes Aristotle appear a "conservative" to us today – indeed, why he is sometimes remembered as the true father of Western conservatism[7] – is that he believed in a

3 See Herbert Storing, *What the Anti-federalists Were For: The Political Thought of the Opponents of the Constitution* (Chicago: University of Chicago Press, 1981) (for a concise treatment of the various Anti-federalist positions).

4 See Louis Hartz, *The Liberal Tradition in America* (New York: Harcourt, Brace & Co., 1955), 78–86 (discussing the relationship between Federalism and liberalism).

5 Russell Kirk devotes the second chapter of his magisterial work on conservative thought to John Adams. Only Edmund Burke took pride of place and is treated in chapter 1. Russell Kirk, *The Conservative Mind* (Chicago: H. Regnery Co., 1953).

6 Aristotle, *Pol.* 1.2.253a20. *The Basic Works of Aristotle* (Richard McKeon, ed., New York: Random House, 1941). Aristotle was no collectivist in the modern sense, of course. He thought the state exists for the benefit of creating the conditions of the good life for the individual, but he also taught that the state was prior to the individual in a *formal* sense – in the sense that the individual apart from the state is not fully human.

7 George F. Will, *Statecraft as Soulcraft: What Government Does* (New York: Simon and Schuster, 1984).

human "telos," an end or an essential human nature.[8] This means that certain forms of social and political institutions will be more "natural" or "correct," from the standpoint of our essential human nature, than others. The "anti-essentialist" attack on the naturalness of certain forms of life and particular forms of social and political institutions has advanced with the liberal tradition and has been part of it from Locke forward.

Two consequences flow from this premodern Aristotelian view of the human condition, whether cast in pagan or Christian form. First, the individual apart from the state is not fully human.[9] It is our social and political life that is literally *constitutive* of our humanity and that gives us our "second nature." It is only in the social condition that we truly become individuals. Second, political authority does not flow from the individual. It flows from the capacity of the state to help us reach our telos. The well-formed individual is the "end" of the state, but the state comes first in a formal sense.[10] True political legitimacy is based on the capacity of the state to help us attain our good, our end – our human telos. Thus, the individual flows from the state, not the state from the individual.

Locke began from exactly the opposite assumption. The individual is prior to the state in the sense that the legitimacy of all of our political and social institutions must be traced to the consent of the individual who is to be governed by these institutions. This means that all political authority flows from the individual. For Locke, this principle was bounded only by the strictures of natural law, which is an emanation of God's will. An individual in the state of nature is not either a "beast or a god," as Aristotle would have had it. He or she is simply a human being possessed of the essential attributes of humanity. We are each born free and equal. We are each rational. We form our political institutions; they do not form us. And these political institutions, which are public in nature, are separate and distinct from all social institutions, including the family.

Locke, in sum, was an "individualist" in the original sense of the term.[11] He was the first political thinker to argue that each of us is possessed of a *right of self-ownership*.[12] We are responsible for our lives and, insofar as each individual

[8] Jonathan Lear, *Aristotle: The Desire to Understand* (Cambridge: Cambridge University Press, 1988) provides an excellent treatment of Aristotle's ethics, politics and metaphysical thought. John Lawrence Hill, *After the Natural Law: How the Classical Worldview Supports Our Modern Moral and Political Values* (San Francisco: Ignatius Press, 2016), 39–46, for an overview of Aristotle's teleology and its relation to virtue ethics.

[9] A human being outside society, he wrote, is "either a beast or a god." Aristotle, *Pol.* 1.2.253a29. He is either less than human or a superhuman who does not need to rely on civilization.

[10] There is a parallel here between Aristotle's metaphysics and his politics. All things, he argued, are a composite of form and matter. Form precedes matter in the sense that material things only exist to the extent that their matter takes a particular form. Similarly, society is the formal cause of our humanity. It shapes our physical nature, making us human beings.

[11] See Steven Lukes, *Individualism* (New York: Harper Torchbooks, 1973) (for an excellent treatment of the varied uses of the concept).

[12] "Though the Earth and all inferior Creatures be common to all Men, yet every Man has a property in his own Person. This no Body has any right to but Himself." John Locke, *Second Treatise of Government*, ed. C. B. McPherson (Indianapolis: Hackett Publishing, 1980), sec. 27. "All of our property rights in the things that we create stem from the right we have in ourselves, and in the fruits of our labor." Ibid.

is inherently rational, we are morally sovereign over ourselves.[13] Each person possesses a general liberty of acting from his own will that prohibits any other person from compelling or coercing him in violation of his natural rights.[14] In sum, the individual is "free" to the extent that he or she understands and acts without coercion. It is the function of the liberal state to walk a fine line: it must provide enough security to protect our rights from the infringement by other individuals, while at the same time it must limit itself from causing its own form of encroachment on the individual.

From this understanding that we own ourselves and our labor, Locke derived his skein of natural rights – the rights to "life, liberty and estates." In the span of just a few pages of the *Second Treatise*, he developed his ideas of property rights as the mixture of a person's labor with the bounty of nature,[15] of the right to equality before the law[16] and the central animating idea of liberalism: the chief end of government is not to promulgate God's will, or to form the character of the good citizen or even to create the just society, but simply to secure the common good and to protect individual rights.[17]

And yet, notwithstanding the individualistic tenor of Locke's philosophy, his outlook remained essentially conservative and premodern in several ways. He was not yet a "liberal" in the contemporary sense of the term. We find in his political thought little of the concern of subsequent liberals with the ways in which *society*, as opposed to *government*, threatens personal freedom. He did not generally criticize tradition, custom or habit, though he began the liberal critique of certain forms of authority, particularly paternal authority.

Nor would Locke have rejected as offensive to the liberal principle laws prohibiting homosexuality, alcohol and drug use, gambling, prostitution, suicide and other putatively self-regarding acts. Unlike modern libertarians, he believed that the power of the legislature extends beyond enforcing individual rights to the protection of the common good. Locke would have had no sympathy with the notion, virtually emblematic of twentieth-century liberalism, that the state has no business "legislating morality": since "[t]he obligations of the natural law cease[] not in society…[for] the law of nature stands as an eternal rule to all men" (sec. 135). Nor did he believe that freedom of expression extends to all opinions: "No opinion contrary to human

13 "We are born free, as we are born rational." Ibid., sec. 61.

14 Ibid., sec. 63.

15 Ibid., sec. 27.

16 Locke's idea of equality was, of course, formal equality, equality before the law. "Though I have said that…that all Men by Nature are equal, I cannot be understood to suppose all sorts of Equality…[but only] the equal right that every man hath to his natural Freedom, without being subjected to the will or authority of any other Man." Ibid., sec. 54.

17 "The great and chief end, therefore, of men's uniting into Commonwealth and putting themselves under Government, is the Preservation of their Property." Ibid., sec. 124. The term "property" here designates *all of our rights*, not simply the rights we have in our material possessions. As one commentator notes, for Locke and his followers in the eighteenth century, we did not have rights in our property, we had property in our rights. John Phillip Reid, *The Concept of Liberty in the American Revolution* (Chicago: University of Chicago Press, 1988), 5, 23–25.

society, or to those moral rules which are necessary to the preservation of civil society, are to be tolerated by the magistrate."[18]

In sum, Locke was a Christian classical liberal, not a secular libertarian.

Today, Locke's philosophy is sometimes most closely associated with economic freedom – with property rights, contractual freedoms and the free market. Indeed, as we will see in Chapter 4, when the Supreme Court began to read what most believed to be "Lockean" values into the Constitution during the early twentieth century, their emphasis was on a right to "freedom of contract" – the freedom of employers and employees to make contracts, without government intervention, into the terms and conditions of the relationship.[19] But economic liberty was not more important to Locke than other personal liberties such as freedom of religion or the general freedom to be left alone to live one's life in peace. Rather, the economic side of Locke's thought came to be emphasized *as a reaction*, beginning in the late nineteenth century, to progressive legislation regulating the economy. To remember Locke as a "possessive individualist" is to distort his message.[20] Locke had a holistic conception of freedom that included, but was certainly not exhausted by, economic freedom.

LIBERALISM'S SECOND WAVE: BENTHAM AND THE UTILITARIANS

Locke died in 1704, seventy years before the American Revolution and at a time when Western thought was in the process of a tumultuous philosophical upheaval. The old natural law tradition and the Christian theological edifice on which it rested were crumbling under the weight of the increasingly skeptical and secular philosophy of the age.[21] By the end of the eighteenth century, a newer brand of thinkers – the utilitarians – ushered in classical liberalism's second phase, grounding liberty on a purely secular footing.[22] Jeremy Bentham, James Mill and their followers rested the case for liberty on the "greatest happiness" principle. Bentham,

[18] *Letter on Toleration.*

[19] The seminal case was *Lochner* v. *New York*, 198 US 45 (1905), in which the Supreme Court struck down a law limiting the number of hours bakers may work.

[20] See e.g. C. B. McPherson, *The Political Theory of Possessive Individualism: Hobbes to Locke* (Oxford: Clarendon Press, 1969).

[21] For a discussion of the breakdown of the natural law tradition and its consequences, see Hill, *After the Natural Law.*

[22] Utilitarianism is a form of moral consequentialism; i.e., what makes an act "good" or "bad" are the beneficial consequences of that act, rather than whether the act is of a kind that has been specifically required or prohibited under some moral principle, as Kant would have defined it. The classic statement is that the good is equivalent to "the greatest happiness of the greatest number," a principle Bentham picked up from Joseph Priestley's *First Principles of Government* (1768) but which had antecedents in the work of Francis Hutcheson and David Hume. In fact, the basic idea goes back to thinkers like Epicurus and Aristippus in antiquity. The appeal of utilitarianism is that it attempts to salvage the idea that moral questions have determinate or objective answers (morality is not purely subjective or relative) while grounding morality on a more secular, this-worldly foundation, i.e., happiness. The classic statement is that the best action is that which maximizes the most happiness for

an agnostic who wrote anti-religious tracts under a pseudonym, famously referred to Locke's God-given natural rights as "nonsense on stilts."[23] He similarly rejected Locke's social contract as pure myth, arguing that government is and must always be founded on power, not consent.

Bentham and the utilitarians placed liberty on an altogether new footing. Guided by the "greatest happiness principle," they held that all values – including freedom – can only be justified if they conduce to "the greatest happiness of the greatest number." The utilitarians continued to use the term "rights" to describe liberty claims, but they used this term in a far more provisional sense than Locke and other natural rights theorists had. Property rights were justified, for example, on the premise that protecting the individual's right to possession of the things he or she owns is conducive to security and to the expansion of social largesse, both of which promote the overall happiness of society. Yet – and here was the implicit assumption which was not drawn by utilitarians until much later – if utility can be maximized by *limiting* property rights in certain ways, then so much for property rights. *Freedom served utility*, not the other way around.

Nevertheless, for most of Bentham's life, utilitarianism led him to many of the same practical conclusions as Locke had drawn. Since the individual tends to know best what will bring personal happiness, it is generally best to leave each individual free to make personal choices. The characteristic classical liberal attitudes opposing paternalism and other forms of intervention rested on an empirical assumption that personal freedom and economic laissez-faire tended to generate more happiness than highly interventionist political systems. During much of the nineteenth-century, freedom and utility were values thought to exist in harmony with each other. This happy marriage began to break down for many utilitarian thinkers toward the end of the nineteenth century with the advent of the progressive era. Indeed, as Bentham grew older, he reconsidered many of his conclusions, favoring more government intervention in areas he had once thought beyond the reach of government.[24]

the most people. Happiness, in turn, is a function of human pleasure, or the absence of pain. A bit rudely put, the "best" action to take in any particular circumstance is the one that creates the most pleasure overall. "Good" and "bad" do not depend on God's will, or natural law or Kantian duties and rights. Jeremy Bentham, *An Introduction to the Principles of Morals and Legislation* (Amherst: Prometheus Books, 1988) (1789) (developing the classic utilitarian themes and arguments). See L. T. Hobhouse, *Liberalism and Other Writings* (1911), ed. James Meadowcroft (Cambridge: Cambridge University Press, 2006), 31–36 (for a discussion of the utilitarian influence on liberal thought, particularly as it opposed the natural rights philosophy of Locke).

[23] Jeremy Bentham, "Anarchical Fallacies: Being an Examination of the Declarations of Rights Issued during the French Revolution," in *The Works of Jeremy Bentham*, vol. 2, ed. John Bowring (Edinburgh: W. Tait, 1843).

[24] As one Bentham commentator has concluded, "there is nothing in Bentham's character, in the principle of utility or in the logic of the [collective] will, to suggest he could not have been a supporter of Fabian socialism had he lived a hundred years later." D. J. Manning, *The Mind of Jeremy Bentham* (London: Longmans, 1968), 97.

If utilitarianism was a potential threat to liberty in this way, it promised greater freedom to the individual in another. Bentham was a secular thinker, an agnostic and a skeptic concerning all of the lingering vestiges of religion in our moral tradition. The trammels of religion served no purpose if they did not promote the greatest happiness of the greatest number, which Bentham equated with the greatest sum of *pleasure* for all individuals. This "hedonic" or pleasure-centric calculus of utilitarianism, along with a general weariness concerning the moral conventions of Christianity, led Bentham to far more anti-moralistic conclusions than Locke had reached.

Bentham was thus among the first to propound a series of positions that we regard today as "liberal" in a broader sense. He argued for the decriminalization of private, consensual activity on the grounds that these activities were often harmless and because laws prohibiting them were often inefficacious.[25] He observed, in opposition to the "eye for an eye" retributive view of punishment, that all punishment is intrinsically evil, even when necessary.[26] He insisted that education is often more efficient than punishment in preventing various forms of mischief.[27] He argued for broader religious toleration that included not simply greater freedom of worship but greater freedom *from* religion.[28] He thought that paternalistic laws were frequently harmful and often pointless.[29] He opposed censorship of almost every kind.[30] And he insisted on reforms of the criminal law suitable to a more enlightened age.[31] In each of these ways, utilitarianism's "this-worldly" influence emphasized happiness, pleasure and self-fulfillment over the sectarian values that lingered within the natural rights tradition.[32]

25 Bentham, *Principles of Morals and Legislation*, chap. 13, sec. 2, 134 "Cases Unmeet for Punishment." In cases where an act "might be, on some occasions, mischievous or disagreeable, but the person whose interest it concerns gave his consent"; Jeremy Bentham, *Of Sexual Irregularities, and Other Writings on Sexual Morality*, eds. P. Schofield, C. Pease-Watkin and M. Quinn (Oxford: Clarendon Press, 2014).

26 Bentham, *Principles of Morals and Legislation*, 70 (sec. 1, ii); ibid., 175 (sec. 4, xiii).

27 Ibid., 177 (sec. 5, xvii).

28 Ibid., 320–21 (sec. I, xvii). Bentham left a substantial bequest to the University of London, now University College London, which he helped found and which was among the first universities to admit Catholics, Jews and atheists.

29 Ibid., 321 (sec. I, xviii). Mill would sharpen this into a general principle later as well.

30 "As to the evil which results from censorship," he wrote, "it is impossible to measure it, because it is impossible to tell where it ends." Jeremy Bentham, *On the Liberty of the Press, and Public Discussion, and other Legal and Political Writings for Spain and Portugal*, eds. C. Pease Watkins and P. Schofield (Oxford: Clarendon Press, 2012).

31 In particular, there are four classes of acts which should never by punished: where punishment is groundless (because no harm had been done), inefficacious (because the act could not be deterred by threat of punishment), unprofitable (because punishment creates more pain than pleasure) or needless (where it can be achieved by other means, such as education). Bentham, *Principles of Morals and Legislation*, 170–78.

32 One pertinent example: Locke had argued that we own our lives and may do with them as we wish. But he drew the line at suicide, arguing that each life was a gift of God that may not be forfeited. Bentham, on the other hand, believed in rational suicide in cases where the quantity of pleasure remaining in one's life was outstripped by the likely pain to be experienced.

Yet, at perhaps the deepest level, Locke and Bentham had two very different understandings of the relationship between law and liberty. Locke was still, after all, a natural law thinker. Even where he parted ways with Aquinas and the Catholic natural law tradition,[33] his worldview was still basically teleological. He agreed with these earlier thinkers that natural law was not restrictive of human nature, but instead furthered it: "law, in its true nature, is not so much the Limitation as *the direction of a free and intelligent agent* to his proper interest."[34] To the extent that positive law reflected natural law, it was a force for good in the life of the individual. In fact, law was *necessary* to freedom, for "where there is no law, there is no freedom" (sec. 57). True liberty is freedom to act within the bounds of, and with the support of, natural law.[35]

Bentham took the opposite view: *law is always constraint, pure and simple.* Laws always diminish freedom. Where there is no law, there is *total* freedom – an insecure freedom, perhaps, but freedom, nonetheless. Law and liberty were for Bentham utterly antithetical commodities. Where, for Locke, the right balance between liberty and restraint is found in *following* natural law, for Bentham and the utilitarians, there was no natural law. The question for utilitarians was one of coordinating clashing desires, balancing the restraints imposed by positive law to achieve the greatest happiness of the greatest number. In sum, freedom, for Bentham, is what Isaiah Berlin called a "negative" concept: freedom means the absence of restraint, and laws – by their very nature – restrain.[36]

Today, Locke and Bentham represent the two pillars of classical liberal thought. They agreed on many of the same conclusions – that the state should be limited, that markets should be free and that religious toleration was essential. Yet, it is with Bentham that we find the beginning of modern, secular liberalism.

TOWARD A THIRD IDEA OF FREEDOM: THE CONTINENTAL INFLUENCE

Five years before Mill published *On Liberty*, in 1854, there appeared in English a translation of Wilhelm von Humboldt's *Ideen zu einem Versuch, die Gränzen der Wirksamkeit des Staates zu bestimmen*, now translated as *The Limits of State Action*.[37] Humboldt, who was the architect of the vaunted Prussian educational system and the

33 For example, Aquinas had taught that human beings possess an innate template for knowing right and wrong: he called this "synderesis," the basis by which the well-formed individual develops a conscience. Locke, as an empiricist, rejected synderesis arguing that we are born *tabula rasa*, blank slates. All morality is learned. Hill, *After the Natural Law*, 115–44 (for a discussion of the breakdown of classical natural law ideas in the early modern period).

34 Locke, *Second Treatise*, sec. 57 (emphasis in original).

35 Locke insisted that "*the end of law* is not to abolish or restrain, but to preserve and enlarge freedom," since the individual can never safely enjoy his rights in the absence of laws. Indeed, freedom is not simply "liberty to do as one lists" (sec. 57).

36 Isaiah Berlin, "Two Concepts of Liberty," in *Four Essays on Liberty* (Oxford: Oxford University Press, 1969).

37 Wilhelm von Humboldt, *The Limits of State Action* (Indianapolis: Liberty Fund, 1993).

founder of the University of Berlin, had written the book as a young man, in 1791–2, but decided not to publish it for political reasons. His brother published the book posthumously in the early 1850s, when it came into Mill's hands. *The Limits of State Action* may well represent the first genuine expression of libertarian thought in the western political tradition.

Coming of age in Prussia at the end of the eighteenth century, Humboldt drew his philosophical inspiration from the mélange of influences dominant among Continental thinkers at that time. In differing ways, these influences saw freedom as considerably more than the purely "negative" idea embraced by the English, particularly in Bentham's form. The term "freedom," of course, is used to refer both to our external political freedoms – our rights and liberties – and our internal capacity to make choices (i.e., the capacity once called "freedom of the will"). Continental thinkers began to connect these two facets of freedom – inner freedom and political liberty – in new ways. They began to see our external political and social freedoms not simply as limits on government power but as necessary conditions for the perfection of freedom in its internal sense.

But what might we mean by "freedom in its internal sense"? What is "freedom of choice," exactly? Continental thinkers including Rousseau, Kant and Fichte laid the groundwork for what Isaiah Berlin referred to as a "positive" idea of freedom – one that connects the sources of external social conditions with the capacity for some form of internal self-control, autonomy, authenticity or even self-realization.[38] Some of these notions pointed in ominous directions. Rousseau, for example, insisted in *The Social Contract* that it might be necessary for people to be "forced to be free" – that true freedom might require a large measure of compulsion. Accordingly, Berlin and other recent thinkers have argued that, pushed far enough, "positive" ideas of freedom lead in the direction of totalitarianism.[39]

But Humboldt drew from a welter of softer influences – influences that agreed that freedom had something to do with self-betterment and human progress while stopping short of more extreme versions of the thesis. From the philosopher and mathematician Leibnitz, Humboldt adopted the idea of the potential perfectibility of man, and from the recent work of the French thinker, Condorcet, the idea that human history was on a progressive course of self-betterment – a course which could be guided and accelerated by humane political institutions. From the romanticism of the *Sturm und Drang* movement came an emphasis on sentiment, the cult of genius and the quest for living authentically from our true inner nature rather than being guided by external social customs and norms.

Perhaps the most important influence on Humboldt, however, came from the writings of Immanuel Kant. In the 1780s, Kant had developed an ethical alternative

[38] Berlin, "Two Concepts of Liberty," 131–34.
[39] Ibid.

to utilitarianism based on a rational foundation of rights and duties owed to others.[40] Central to Kant's ethical thought was the idea of autonomy. Kantian autonomy was not simply the idea (as some use the term today) that the individual should have the right to do as he wishes. Rather, Kant argued that autonomy consisted of giving oneself a law, grounded in reason, by which one should live.[41] True autonomy requires that one's acts not be influenced by (heteronomous) emotions but, instead, by reason alone. Kant also concluded (in the most important version of his categorical imperative) that every human being should be treated as an end-in-himself – as autonomous and worthy of dignity and respect.[42]

In the eclectic spirit of these influences, Humboldt wrote, "the true end of Man… is the highest and most harmonious development of his powers to a complete and consistent whole." He went on to say that achieving this goal requires two conditions – freedom and "a variety of situations."[43] The thrust of Humboldt's argument was to provide a thoroughly *individualized* conception of state power. No legal prohibition is permissible "when the advantage or disadvantage refers only to the State itself." In other words, the state has no interest in creating or enforcing "the common good," whatever that might mean. Legal prohibitions are only justified when one person's act "encroach[es] on [another's] rights." Whereas Mill would later frame these limits on individual action in quasi-utilitarian terms using the idea of "harm," Humboldt saw them in terms of rights. Yet, he was not speaking of natural rights, but of rights in a more conventional sense: a right can only be infringed "when someone is deprived of a part of what properly belongs to him, or of his personal freedom, without his consent or against his will."[44]

Humboldt argued, as Bentham had, against purely religious and moralistic justifications for laws that limit liberty. Assaults on virtue, the performance of acts that create a bad example for others and even intentional attempts to corrupt are beyond the power of the state to reprove. "According to these principles, we cannot assume the injustice of any actions which only create offence, and especially as regards

40 In contrast to utilitarian thinkers such as Bentham and Mill, who thought that the goodness of an action depends on which act generates the best consequences (i.e., the most happiness or pleasure), Kant's thought was deontological or duty-based. For Kant, the ethical quest depends not on generating the most "good" but about doing what is "right," which requires following certain laws of reason which ground our ethical duties. Immanuel Kant, *Grounding for the Metaphysics of Morals in Kant's Ethical Philosophy* (Indianapolis: Hackett Publishing, 1983). See Allen W. Wood, *Kant's Ethical Thought* (Cambridge: Cambridge University Press, 1999) (for an excellent introduction and overview of Kant's ethical theory).

41 Autonomy is literally "self-rule." The autonomous person is "free as regards all laws of nature and… obeys only those laws he gives to himself." Kant, *Grounding for the Metaphysics of Morals*, bk. 1, sec. 2. *Kant's Ethical Philosophy*, trans. James W. Ellington, 1983.

42 The second iteration of Kant's categorical imperative was to "always treat humanity, whether in your own person or the person of any other, never simply as a means, but always at the same time, as an end."

43 Humboldt, *Limits of State Action*, 10.

44 Ibid., 87.

religion and morals." Continuing, he concluded that "[h]e who does anything to wound the conscience or moral sense of others may indeed act immorally, but, so long as he is not guilty of being importunate, he violates no right."[45] Even a possible exposure to putatively demoralizing influences – witnessing an offensive or violent action, or listening to a discussion calculated to harm the virtue of the listener or mislead the reason and sound sense of others – would not be sufficient to justify restrictions on freedom.

Mill had read many of the authors who influenced this tradition including those, like Fichte and Hegel, who wrote after Humboldt. But Humboldt's book had a galvanizing influence upon him. It encapsulated many of the same conclusions toward which Mill had been moving. Humboldt's ideas gave freedom a new footing – one that dovetailed with Mill's embrace of romanticism, individualism and antimoralism. And Mill dutifully credited Humboldt by quoting him in the epigraph of *On Liberty*, by singling him out in his *Autobiography* and by mentioning Humboldt half a dozen times in the text of *On Liberty*.[46] Mill had recently read Humboldt when he wrote to Harriet from Rome in January 1855:

> I came back to an idea that we have talked about & thought that the best thing to write & publish at present would be a volume on Liberty.[47]

45 Ibid., 88.

46 The epigraph of *On Liberty* quoted from Humboldt reads, "The grand, leading principle toward which every argument unfolded in these pages directly converges, is the absolute and essential importance of human development in its richest diversity." See "Editor's Introduction," *Limits of State Action*, xviii, n. 4, 5, for discussion of Mill's references to Humboldt.

47 Mill to Harriet (January 15, 1855), *CW*, 14:294.

3

Inventing Modern Liberalism

In contrast to John Rawls, Richard Rorty and other important contemporary liberal philosophers who have tried to build a wall of separation between politics and philosophy,[1] Mill thought that our political and economic conclusions had to rest on a firm philosophical foundation. One's worldview mattered to one's politics. This is why he had written his *System of Logic* first – to lay the foundation for what he thought would come later. In this respect, at least, Mill was closer to Aristotle than to Rawls.[2]

Yet where his liberalism is concerned, Mill's philosophical foundations reflect a welter of conflicting influences. He was an empiricist who was drawn to romanticism, a libertarian with increasingly socialist sympathies and – perhaps the deepest tension of all in his thought – a philosophical determinist who valorized, above all other ideals, freedom of choice.[3] In the opening lines of *On Liberty*, he dismissed Lockean natural rights while parting ways from the utilitarianism of Bentham and his father. Yes, the case for liberty was based on utility – but utility only "in the largest sense, *grounded in the permanent interests of man as a progressive being*."[4]

[1] Rawls argued that "comprehensive doctrines" – his term for an overarching worldview, whether it is religious or philosophical – cannot play a role in liberal political societies. All arguments in the liberal mainstream must be limited by "public reason." John Rawls, *Political Liberalism* (New York: Columbia University Press, extended edition, 2005), 58–61. "Political liberalism does not engage those who want... the whole truth." Ibid., 441. See also Richard Rorty, *Contingency, Irony and Solidarity* (Cambridge: Cambridge University Press, 1989) (for an "ironistic" account of liberalism).

[2] In sum, Mill was a "foundationalist," as was almost every important political thinker of his time. In contrast, many twentieth-century thinkers are anti-foundationalist.

[3] I explore the conflict between Mill's basic philosophical assumptions, particularly his determinism and skepticism about the idea of an enduring self or subject, with the tenor of *On Liberty*, which seems to require a belief in a self, and in some conception of free will, in John Lawrence Hill, Theism, Naturalism and Liberalism: John Stuart Mill and the "Final Inexplicability" of the Self, 39 *Pepperdine Law Review* 1401 (2013).

[4] John Stuart Mill, "On Liberty," in *Essays on Politics and Society Part I*, CW, 18:224.

But what might this mean?

Mill's well-considered views on religion, in general, and Christianity, in particular, set the stage for his, and for modern, liberalism. He wrote his most important essay on the topic of God and religion, "Theism," toward the end of his life.[5] Following Comte, who had written that the laws of history entail a progression from religious belief to metaphysics to science, Mill thought it likely that orthodox religion was "destined to disappear" at the hands of progress and secularization.[6]

He proceeded in the essay to subject every aspect of orthodox Christian belief to withering analysis. He trashed the immortality of the soul as a deluded form of wishful thinking – for who, he asked, would really want to live forever? He excoriated the account of the miracles in the Bible and he attacked the traditional philosophical arguments for God's existence. But he ended on an agnostic note, which left some of his more hard-headed friends such as Alexander Bain in disgust. That there might exist an impersonal God of the Philosophers, a cosmic ordering force in Nature, he thought possible – though the evidence falls far short of proof and amounts "only to one of the lower degrees of probability."[7]

But as for the personal God of Christianity – a God who is omniscient, omnipotent and supremely good – Mill had only contempt: "The notion of a providential government by an omnipotent Being for the good of his creatures must be entirely dismissed," he wrote.[8] He was more than doubtful about the divinity of Christ but was deeply impressed with Jesus's character and wisdom and gave him high marks as an enlightened moral sage:

> But about the life and sayings of Jesus there is a stamp of personal originality combined with profundity of insight which ... must place the Prophet of Nazareth, even in the estimation of those who have no belief in his inspiration, in the very first rank of men of sublime genius of whom our species can boast. When this pre-eminent genius is combined with the qualities of probably the greatest moral reformer and martyr to that mission, who ever existed upon earth, religion cannot be said to have made a bad choice in pitching on this man as the ideal representative and guide of humanity.[9]

Mill hoped that religious spirit would find its proper object in humanity itself – that there might be a "religion of humanity." As he had once written to August Comte, "I always saw ... in the idea of Humanity, the only one capable of replacing God.

5 "Theism," which was written between 1868 and 1870, was written to follow two other essays he had written in the 1850s – "Nature" and "The Utility of Religion." All three essays are assembled in volume 10 of Mill's *Collected Works*.

6 Ibid., 430.

7 Ibid., 482.

8 Ibid., 482.

9 Ibid., 487–88.

But there is still a long way from this speculation and belief to the manifest feeling I experience today – that it is fully valid, and that the inevitable substitution is at hand."[10]

Rejecting a theological foundation for politics meant that any transcendent concept of human rights based on a belief in God had to be rejected out-of-hand. Mill agreed with Bentham that political thought had to be liberated from the trammels of natural law, natural right and religion in general. Liberalism needed a secular foundation but one that could inspire the quasi-spiritual quest for human progress and self-individuation. Utility provided a serviceable alternative: "good" and "bad" could now be defined in terms of human happiness – the greatest happiness of the greatest number.

But utilitarianism had its own problems. Mill's reverence for Bentham was limited. He had grown up knowing the master, and had acted as Bentham's secretary while still in his teens, but soon grew out of his youthful attachment to Benthamism. That Mill may have associated the arid and anti-individualistic implications of utilitarianism with his nervous breakdown is more than likely. He wrote in his essay on Bentham after the latter's death that Bentham was "not a great philosopher, but a great reformer in philosophy" – a "subversive thinker in an age which has lost all that they could subvert."[11] But he was "a boy to the last," a "one eyed man" who saw only half the truth, though he saw it more clearly than others.[12] Bentham had been, Mill concluded, untouched throughout his life by true passion or grief – rambunctious, impetuous, fearless but lacking in sympathy and marred by "a deficiency of imagination."[13]

There were, of course, well-known philosophical problems with harmonizing utilitarianism with liberty. As Bentham made clear in his writings, there were no real "rights." Any "right that conflicted with achieving the overall happiness of the community would have to be jettisoned. Liberty claims were subordinate to utility claims, and when the two values conflicted, utility trumped liberty.

Equally problematic, Mill charged that utility could not be "cashed out" as the lowest common denominator. Bentham had promised, in essence, that we could retain the notion that there are objective moral truths, as Christian moralists had always taught, but grounded these truths on the more terrestrial ground of collective human happiness. Bentham equated happiness with maximizing pleasure and minimizing pain. Utility as pleasure was a fungible commodity: all values, virtues and courses of action are theoretically reducible to the same lowest common

[10] Linda C. Reader, *John Stuart Mill and the Religion of Humanity* (Columbia: Missouri University Press, 2002).
[11] John Stuart Mill, "Bentham," in *Essays on Ethics, Religion and Society*, *CW*, 10:83, 80.
[12] Ibid., 92.
[13] Ibid., 90.

denominator: the overall pleasure of the community. Thus, Bentham promised that utilitarianism could provide the foundation for a moral science, that all great social and political questions could theoretically be boiled down to questions about how to maximize human happiness. All qualitative questions concerning the relative value of different activities could be reduced to one purely quantitative foundation. This was the import of his quip that, when the quantity of two pleasures are equal, "pushpin is as good as poetry." The only measure of the worth of any action, or value or social policy was its utility, the capacity to generate pleasure (or avoid pain) for those affected by the action.

But this was exactly where Mill parted ways from Bentham. He rejected Bentham's hedonic calculus altogether: there is, Mill insisted, an irreducibly *qualitative* element to utility. Some pleasures are simply "higher" and more valuable than others.[14] Higher pleasures are to be preferred, even if the quantity of the lower pleasure far exceeds that of the higher. A pleasure was "higher," Mill wrote, when it is preferred by all or most persons who are "competently acquainted with both."[15]

So, utility was a kind of heuristic guide for Mill. Of course our prudential judgments about how to act and which laws to enact must be governed by human happiness but Bentham's idea of utility was "much too complex or indefinite an end to be sought except through the medium of various secondary ends."[16] In other words, rules, values and norms have an important role to play in guiding human actions though these must, in turn, be grounded on the general idea of utility.[17] As he had argued in his *System of Logic*, the functions of social scientists and law-making had to be performed in the spirit of an artist. Truth is many-sided, and moral judgment is ultimately a practical art, though an art guided by the general idea of human happiness.

Yet if utility served as a heuristic template, the substance of Mill's liberalism was rooted in the idealism, romanticism and progressivism of Humboldt and the Continental thinkers. Nineteenth-century romanticism, in particular,

[14] "It would be absurd that, in estimating all other things, quality is considered, as well as quantity, while the estimation of pleasure should be supposed to depend on quantity alone." Mill, *Utilitarianism*, CW, 10:211.

[15] Ibid., 211. Thus, Mill was a utilitarian only in the most extended sense of the word. As. C. L. Ten put it, only when we recognize that Mill's is a "hierarchical, pluralistic and essentially non-hedonistic" utilitarianism can it be squared with the argument in *On Liberty*. C. L. Ten, "Mill's Defense of Liberty," in *J. S. Mill, On Liberty in Focus*, eds. John Gray and G. W. Smith (London: Routledge, 1991), 236.

[16] Mill, *Utilitarianism*, chap. II deals specifically with this issue.

[17] Mill was a "rule utilitarian," rather than an "act utilitarian." Moral rules are chosen for their general tendency to promote happiness but they should be followed even where, in a particular instance, there may be some doubt about a rule's utility-promoting function in a particular circumstance. Act utilitarian thinkers such as Bentham, on the other hand, hold that each action must be evaluated on its own terms (e.g., that good rules, which promote bad consequences in a particular case, should be disregarded).

was a reaction against the rationalism of eighteenth-century thought of which utilitarianism was one of the clearest expressions. Romanticism valorized the individual over the collective, imagination over reason, the aesthetic over the moral dimensions of human existence, spontaneity over the collar of habit and tradition, and authenticity over the regimentation of assigned roles. Above all the romantics exalted the genius – the boundary-transcending individual whose example explodes the narrow confines of bourgeois society.[18] These were some of the same influences that had influenced Humboldt. But Humboldt wrote his book in the 1790s. Mill was powerfully influenced by many who came after – by the romantic poets and writers – Wordsworth and Shelley, Coleridge and Carlyle, Byron and Keats – as well by such idealist philosophers as Fichte, Kant, Hegel and Schelling.[19]

These poets and thinkers rejected the empiricism of Locke and Hume and the rationalism of Descartes and Kant, along with the religious orthodoxy which these latter thinkers had supplanted. They rejected it all and drew instead from a dizzying welter of eclectic philosophies. From Rousseau they borrowed the notion that natural man is beneficent at heart, and that our natural goodness is only warped and corrupted by the trammels of social convention. From the German idealists such as Fichte they inherited the notion that the uniqueness of the individual is one with genius and that the development of the authentic self is the most pressing ethical imperative on the individual. From Gnosticism they took the insight that the profoundest spiritual truths are buried in the depths of the human soul and that all customs, rules, habits and conventions are obstructions to the unfolding of the true self.

These influences permeated the intellectual atmosphere of Europe in the late eighteenth and early nineteenth centuries. Humboldt had been influenced by them in the early 1790s, but by the time of Mill's youth, there had been a mushrooming of romantic poets and idealist thinkers – some progressive and some reactionary, some communal and others highly individualistic. Ralph Waldo Emerson, who had given up his Unitarian ministry to embrace a similar mélange of romanticism, idealism and Buddhism, met Mill on Emerson's first visit to England in the mid-1830s. Mill, in turn, introduced him to Carlyle from whom Emerson distilled his own Americanized version of Carlyle's hero-worship. The hero was the self-made man, the "unique," the true individual who never

[18] Isaiah Berlin, *The Roots of Romanticism* (Princeton: Princeton University Press, 2013), 1–20 (for an excellent intellectual history of romanticism); Charles Taylor, *Sources of the Self* (Cambridge: Cambridge University Press, 1989), 393–494 (for a discussion of romanticism and its influence on contemporary culture and morality). Michael Ferber, *Romanticism: A Very Short Introduction* (Oxford: Oxford University Press, 2010).

[19] Nicholas Capaldi, *John Stuart Mill: A Biography* (Oxford: Oxford University Press, 2004), 88–101, for a discussion of these influences on Mill's thought.

acts from imitation. Emerson's essay, "Self-Reliance," written in 1848, was wildly influential among Americans and it captures something of the spirit of the age:

> To believe your own thoughts, to believe that what is true for you in your private heart is true for all men – that is genius. Speak your latent conviction, and it shall be the universal sense, for the inmost in due time becomes the outmost, and our first thought is rendered back to us by the trumpets of the Last Judgment.[20]

Emerson extolled his hearers to "insist on yourself, never imitate ... Every great man is a unique."[21]

These ideas would have sickened Bentham and the elder Mill, perhaps even more than the religion for which they were a substitute – at least the old-time believers were honest fools. And while Mill himself was far too analytical to accept romanticism as a philosophical creed – he pointedly dismissed Emerson's transcendentalism as warmed-over religion – he was drawn, nevertheless, to romanticism's exaltation of the individual and the values of authenticity, self-development and self-expression. *On Liberty* was thus born of the unsteady marriage of utilitarianism and romanticism, of the greatest good for the greatest number, however "progressively" this might be defined, and libertarian individualism.

LIBERALISM AND POSITIVISM

But there was yet another element in Mill's liberalism – an element that cut quite clearly against the grain of his romanticism, even as his romanticism cut against the grain of his utilitarianism. For Mill was, at the end of the day, a positivist – and a fairly radical positivist at that.

Positivism is a highly refined version of empiricism, the view that all knowledge comes through the senses. Stricter forms of empiricism rule out the idea that human beings are born possessing certain kinds of innate knowledge. We have no inborn moral conscience, no innate understanding of basic truths, no inborn intuition that can guide us in our lives. Everything we know, or think, or believe has come to us from experience.

Empiricism and liberalism are the twin arms of the project of modernity, one epistemological, the other political. It is no coincidence that John Locke was not only the first liberal thinker, but the first empiricist as well. His *Essay Concerning Human Understanding* – published the same year as his *Second Treatise* but in many respects completely incompatible with it – is regarded by philosophers as the first

[20] Ralph Waldo Emerson, "Self-Reliance," in *Selected Essays, Lectures and Poems* (New York: Bantam Books, 1990), 148.
[21] Ibid., 168.

systematic defense of modern empiricism.[22] Though Locke was a Christian thinker, he drew several conclusions in his *Essay*, which ran against the tenor of earlier religious thought. The thrust of his empiricism undercut notions of the soul, of free will and even of the natural law. And where previous thinkers concluded that we are born knowing certain truths intuitively – Descartes, for example, claimed that we know God exists by a naked act of introspection – Locke rejected these appeals to intuition. Subsequent empiricists – Bishop Berkeley, David Hume and Mill himself – drew increasingly skeptical conclusions about our knowledge of God, moral truth and the world. This skepticism has under girded the liberal tradition ever since.

Mill's philosophical positions, developed in his *System of Logic*, were thus developments of this earlier tradition, especially David Hume's skeptical empiricism. The *System of Logic*, Mill's first work, was an attempt to "get it right," philosophically before moving on with the more "applied" political and economic questions. In this multivolume treatise, which took him thirteen years to write, he took on every major philosophical problem and movement, discussing everything from the experimental method in science to logical fallacies to the "mind-body problem" and to the problem of free will and determinism. He discussed in what sense morality could be made a science and devoted the better part of one volume to the science of "ethology," Mill's term for sociology. It was here that he began the exploration of the social causes of human behavior and to question age-old assumptions about the "innate" differences based on gender, race and class.

The underlying epistemological thrust of the *Logic* was to defend an *inductive* account of knowledge. All knowledge comes by building up particular sense experiences into greater truths. But there are no "necessary truths" except those that are necessary by convention (i.e., because we define terms in a certain way to make them true). The more traditional view he was attacking – known as "intuitionism" or, as Mill called it, the "innate principle metaphysics" – was often the foundation for political conservatism. Those who hold intuitionist views believe that we can know certain basic truths or "innate principles" through an act of reflection or intuition. No prior experience is necessary to have this knowledge. The principles that we know by intuition, moreover, have the status of necessary truths. They are true in an a priori way – not by experience, but by necessity or logic. Most importantly, and controversially, the intuitionist holds that the "obviousness" of these principles is their pedigree, the very proof that they must be true. These were the positions Mill was attacking.

Mill's last important philosophical work, his *Examination of Sir William Hamilton's Philosophy*, published in 1865, developed many of the themes of the

[22] See Hill, *After the Natural Law*, 132–39 (for a discussion of the tensions and conflicts between the empiricism of the *Essay* and the natural law theory of the *Second Treatise*).

Logic but it was written, in part, for polemical purposes. Mill attacked not only the innate principle metaphysics, which Hamilton had defended, but also its political effects. The "innate principle" philosophy, he wrote, has a "tendency so agreeable to human indolence, as well as to conservative interests generally."[23] To put it bluntly, innate principles are usually a foil for religious intolerance and social prejudice.

The intuitionist, Mill charged, tends to take the "obviousness" or strongly felt nature of certain social beliefs – e.g. that the two sexes have different functions in life, that certain forms of sexual activity are inherently wrong – as evidence of their truth. As a conservative writer suggested in our own time, the ordinary man's "indignation, intolerance and disgust" at homosexuality, prostitution and other moral affronts to decency are the strongest evidence that these activities are actually wrong and should be prohibited.[24] But Mill argued that, not only are our feelings not as sure a guide to moral truth as the intuitionists would have it, many of the "obvious" or "innate" characteristics of women, "inferior" races and the lower social classes are the result of social conditions and the social conditioning of the observer – rather than being the result of *real* differences between different individuals.

The implications for liberalism are significant. A commitment to liberty requires the individual to strain against time-honored traditions, habits and customs – both because they do not embody the kinds of innate truths they are sometimes thought to hold, and because these same cultural patterns are imposed, coercive and destructive of the kind of individual experimentation necessary to self-individuation and collective social transformation. They prevent the individual from pursuing his or her own unique style of life, stifling individual development and "freezing" social progress.

To the extent that tradition is usually grounded on the "obvious" character of age-old customs and beliefs and the view that these are rooted in their necessary or essential social character, it is not as sure a guide to human well-being as conservatives think it is.

In sum, Mill's liberalism was a three-pronged affair: his utilitarianism was the template that linked freedom and individualism to social progress and the maximization of happiness, his empiricism was a solvent used to dissolve the external sources of social authority that once limited individual liberty, and his romanticism provided a theory of the substance of freedom – of what freedom really is.

[23] Mill, *Autobiography*, CW, 1:270.

[24] Patrick Devlin, *The Enforcement of Morality* (London: Oxford University, Press, 1963), 17. Devlin was criticizing the British Wolfenden Report, which had advocated the decriminalization of homosexuality and prostitution. His attack led to a response by H. L. A. Hart who, in essence, stood in for Mill in defending a liberal approach to these activities. H. L. A. Hart, *Law, Liberty and Morality* (London: Oxford University Press, 1964).

THE HEART OF LIBERTY

The spiritual heart of *On Liberty* is Chapter III, titled, "Of Individuality as One of the Elements of Well-Being."[25] Here Mill developed his theory of the relationship between freedom, self-development and progress. Our individual natures are often in conflict with social conventions and traditions. The latter can overwhelm us. The undeveloped self is distinct from, and frequently in tension with, social influences, along with the residue of tradition, custom and habit that threaten its emergence:

> A person whose desires are his own – are the expression of his own nature, as it has been developed and modified by his own culture – is said to have a character. One whose desires and impulses are not his own has no character any more than a steam engine has a character.[26]

There is almost an organic and natural character to the true self: "Human nature is not a machine to be built after a model, and set to do exactly the work prescribed for it, but a tree, which requires to grow and develop itself on all sides, according to the tendency *of the inward forces which make it a living thing.*"[27]

Again, we find, even in these brief passages, that Mill was drawing together divergent, often conflicting, philosophical traditions concerning the self – from the Renaissance humanists, from post-Kantian idealists and from the romantic thinkers whom he claimed saved him after his nervous breakdown. In the spirit of the great humanists of the Renaissance, he insisted that "among the works of man which human life is rightly employed in beautifying and perfecting, the first in importance surely is man himself."[28] From the mélange of idealism and romanticism that influenced so much of nineteenth-century thought, he insisted that self-development, individuality and genius were largely one and the same thing. "Individuality is the same thing with development ... it is only the cultivation of individuality which produces, or can produce, well-developed human beings."[29]

At the core of his idea of freedom is the notion that choice-making is essential to becoming *an individual*. To be free is to choose, and choosing is literally *constitutive* of our individuality. Thus, freedom is not valuable simply in an instrumental way as the means for satisfying particular desires, as it was for Bentham. It is the means of self-creation. Choices possess a profound moral significance. Through them, we cultivate our capacity for judgment and decision-making:

> The human faculties of judgment, perception, discriminative feeling, mental activity and even moral preference are exercised only in making a choice. He who

25 Mill, *On Liberty*, CW, 18:260.
26 Ibid., 264.
27 Ibid., 263 (my emphasis).
28 Ibid., 264.
29 Ibid., 267.

> does anything because it is the custom makes no choice. He gains no practice either in discerning or in desiring what is best. The mental and the moral, like the muscular powers, improve only by being used.[30]

It is through our choices that we *literally construct ourselves*.[31]

In sum, Mill *re-conceptualized our very idea of freedom*. The classical liberal idea of negative liberty, freedom as non-interference by the government, was a *necessary* but not a *sufficient* condition for individual freedom. True freedom requires not only non-interference into the private choices of the individual, but that one's will is *one's own*, that it is the expression of one's autonomous inner self and not merely the product of social influences.[32] Although he did not quite put it in such concrete terms, for Mill, the fullest flowering of freedom entails that each individual has the opportunity to discover, develop and express his essential character – his core authentic individual self.

Freedom as self-development, then, meant that we must be on guard against the "tyranny of the majority." Mill followed Tocqueville in warning that the problem of the tyranny of the majority was far worse in a democracy than in other forms of government. In fact, in a democracy, *social* tyranny was likely to be far more dangerous to freedom than *political* tyranny, for social tyranny penetrates the innermost recesses of the self:

> when society is itself the tyrant… its means of tyrannizing are not restricted to the acts which it may do by the hands of its political functionaries. Society can and does execute its own mandates and [when it does] it practices a social

[30] Ibid., 262.

[31] Ibid., 225–26.

[32] In contrast to the "negative" idea of freedom, Mill's is a positive, mildly perfectionistic and more individualistic idea of freedom. As commentators have observed, this is a "positive" idea of freedom to the extent that freedom requires more than non-interference and depends on the realization of other internal values – autonomy, integrity, prudence. Indeed, as one commentator has put it, "some of Mill's critics have suspected that the relationship he has argued for among liberty, self-development and happiness are no more than a series of analytic equivalencies." John Gray, *Mill, On Liberty: A Defense* (London: Routledge and Kegan Paul, 1983), 14. Mill's concept of freedom is mildly perfectionistic to the extent that freedom is connected to the realization of virtue. Sounding more like Aristotle than Bentham, in his *System of Logic*, he concluded his argument for the possibility of human freedom with the words: "And hence it is said with truth, that none but a person of confirmed virtue is completely free." John Stuart Mill, *System of Logic*, *CW*, 8:841. Finally, it is a more individualistic idea of freedom in the sense that freedom is now connected to a specifically individual virtue – self-realization. Freedom, in sum, is not merely a condition in which the unformed and unfinished individual is at liberty to act as he desires. It is a deeply value-laden idea: to be free is to be able to act in accordance with one's own essential nature as it has been developed and refined through choice-making. See John Lawrence Hill, "Mill, Freud and Skinner: The Concept of the Self and the Moral Psychology of Liberty," *Seton Hall Law Review* 1995; 26(1): 92, 126–30 (comparing Mill's concept of freedom and the self with Freudian and behavioristic theories of human psychology).

> tyranny more formidable than many forms of political oppression since ... it leaves fewer means of escape, penetrating much more deeply into the details of life and enslaving the soul itself.[33]

Finally, Mill insisted that we should be vigilant concerning the self-reinforcing nature of custom and tradition, their tendency to cast merely fortuitous social patterns into the form of "obvious truths" and unassailable practices. In each of these ways, non-political forms of coercion and conformity were far more dangerous to individuality than political power.

This was not, of course, the view of classical liberals who were closer, in this respect, to Aristotle and the conservatism of the pre-modern tradition. This older philosophy taught that tradition and social custom were essential not only to social cohesion but to the healthy formation of individual character.[34] Yet, this sanguine view of society began to change with Rousseau and later romantic thinkers who, in turn, influenced Mill. It was Rousseau who insisted that modern society was a corrupting force on the natural goodness of the individual and which gives us a life, as he put it with the characteristic *panache*, of "honor without virtue, reason without wisdom and pleasure without happiness."[35] But where Rousseau believed that modern society was a threat to our moral character, Mill thought it was the bane of our individuality. His attitude only seems to have deepened – indeed, to have been scorched and sealed within the sinews of his life and thought – by his and Harriet's treatment at the hands of Victorian society during their twenty-year friendship. He warned his readers that "society has now fairly got the better of individuality and the danger which now threatens human nature is not the excess, but the deficiency, of personal impulses and preferences."[36]

In fact, not only did tradition and custom cloud out the prospects for exercising what Mill called "the right and duty of self-development," they threatened social progress itself: "Where not the person's own character but the traditions and customs of other people are the rule of conduct, there is wanting one of the principle ingredients of human happiness, and quite the chief ingredient of individual and social progress."[37] In sum, when society controls the individual, the individual will simply reflect society's values, and when this happens, genuine social transformation is impossible. When social forces control the individual, society itself stagnates.

33 Mill, *On Liberty*, *CW*, 18:219–20. Mill's passion swells in passages such as this, where he is warning of the "tyranny of the majority." Indeed, Mill had imbibed his Tocqueville, who coined that phrase.

34 For pre-modern thinkers, the individual outside of society is not naturally free or autonomous. As Hannah Arendt points out, our word "idiot" comes from the Greek "idiota," which meant not a mentally deficient person, but someone without any real sense of himself as a human being. Hannah Arendt, *The Human Condition* (New York: Doubleday and Company, 1958).

35 Jean-Jacques Rousseau, *Discourse on the Origin of Inequality*, in *The Social Contract and the Discourses*, trans. G. D. H. Cole (New York: Washington Square Press, 1973), 116.

36 Mill, *On Liberty*, *CW*, 18:264.

37 Ibid., 261.

Thus, human progress depends on individual freedom and individual self-discovery. We need more "experiments in living," which will permit future generations to evaluate and compare various lifestyles to decide which are most conducive to happiness, self-development and progress. There is a distinctly Darwinian strain to this argument. The social equivalent of Darwin's "chance variation and natural selection" is brought about by freedom: free choice conduces to a diversity of lifestyles, which in turn, will propel social evolution. *On Liberty*, we should remember, was published in 1859, the same year as Darwin's *Origin of the Species*. These ideas were perhaps "in the air" at this time.

It was the essential constellation of modern liberal ideals – happiness, individuality, diversity, self-development and the quest for social progress – that were linked together and then arrayed against the forces of convention and custom, habit and tradition. It was here that liberalism assumed its modern *anti-conservative* guise and that individualism came to be opposed to traditionalism.

MILL'S RADICALISM

John Stuart Mill holds an ambiguous place in the liberal tradition. He is frequently remembered today as a kind of proto-libertarian, a classical liberal who pushed the case for freedom beyond the protection of property rights to encompass the realm of more "personal" freedoms. There is some truth in this picture, but it is only a partial truth. Certainly, his bona fides as a proto-libertarian are established by his defense of the harm principle, which protects a zone of private activity (Chapter 5), his encomia to freedom of speech (Chapter 6) and his warnings about collective power. Had our own current issues been at the forefront of public debate in his day, he would have defended a right to abortion, legalized marijuana and other drugs, a virtually unlimited right to divorce and the right of the dying to engage in assisted suicide. He would have ardently supported racial and gender equality (Chapter 7). And though it might be anachronistic to project modern issues back onto Mill and his time, if he were participating in the contemporary debates concerning LGBT rights, there can be little doubt that he would have defended equality on the basis of sexual orientation and gay marriage.

The rudiments of these various positions, all defended in *On Liberty*, are standard libertarian faire today. It is little wonder that those who are only familiar with *On Liberty* would find in Mill's thought an early version of libertarianism. Yet when we look beyond *On Liberty*, we see that Mill's positions on politics, history, economics and the nature of human progress place him well outside the classical liberal and libertarian mainstream. They make him, indeed, the harbinger and theoretical architect of progressive liberalism and, in some respects, augur positions well to the left of contemporary progressivism.

One of the most striking things about Mill's philosophy – and what makes him so difficult to "pigeon-hole" as a political thinker – is that he held fairly radical positions at higher levels of principle, but frequently drew more conservative positions at the level of application. The source of his radicalism lay precisely in the influence of the socialism and idealism of the Continental school.

Mill accepted the St. Simonian thesis that civilization progresses through "organic" and "critical" periods, the former consisting of a period of widespread acceptance of some general truth or creed, until this truth is outgrown, followed by a "critical" period characterized by skepticism and the dissolution of this consensus – until another organic period arises. In this way, history moves in a kind of upward spiral, cyclically yet progressively, "until the triumph of a yet more advanced creed" ushers in a new and higher organic period.[38] Greek and Roman polytheism, for example, was followed by the rise of pre-Christian philosophers, who were more rational and skeptical, which was followed again by the organic period of Christianity. Mill concluded that this roughly fifteen hundred year organic Christian period had ended with the Reformation, which led in turn, to the resurgence of rational philosophy in the seventeenth and eighteenth centuries – a period that still persists today.

Mill was similarly influenced by Comte's still more progressive conception of history according to which human civilization goes through three stages: the theological, the metaphysical and the "positive" or scientific stages. The theological stage culminated with Catholicism and feudalism; the metaphysical, in which abstract doctrines of human rights replaced theological conceptions of the human condition, spanned the period from the Reformation through the French Revolution. The "positive" phase, as Mill saw it, had yet to arrive, or perhaps was dawning in his own time. Yet he hoped, as Hegel did, that there was soon to be a final resolution, a culminating synthesis – an end to progressive history in which a form of liberal socialism would reign:

> I looked forward, through the present age of loud disputes but generally weak convictions, to a future which shall unite the best qualities of the critical with the best qualities of the organic periods; unchecked liberty of thought, unbounded freedom of individual action in all modes not hurtful to others; but also convictions as to what is right and wrong, useful and pernicious deeply engraven on the feelings by early education and general unanimity of sentiment, and so firmly grounded in reason and in the true exigencies of life, that they shall not, like all former and present creeds, religions, ethical and political, require to be periodically thrown off and replaced by others.[39]

How far Mill distanced himself from the classical liberalism of his father's generation is clear in his *Autobiography*, where he says that, through the socialist writers, his "eyes were opened to the very limited and temporary value of the old political

[38] Mill, *Autobiography*, CW, 1:170.
[39] Ibid., 172.

economy, which assumes private property and inheritance as indefensible facts, and freedom of production and exchange as the *dernier mot* of social improvement."[40] He forcefully rejected the egoistic conception of human nature that had dominated English thought from Hobbes through Bentham and which had been central to classical liberal ideas. Like civilization itself, the human mind must go through a certain order of "possible progress, in which some things must precede others ... [so that] all questions of political institutions are relative, not absolute and that different stages of human progress not only will have, but *ought* to have, different institutions."[41]

His commitments to socialism only grew deeper with time. In the *Autobiography*, he ardently wished that "Owenite, St. Simonian and all other anti-property doctrines might spread widely among the poorer classes."[42] He applauded the boldness with which the socialist writers and the St. Simonians, in particular, had begun to attack the traditional family, which needed "more alteration than remains to be made in any other great social institution." And he hoped that socialism could bring society "closer to some ideal standard."[43]

Gradually, Mill moved toward socialism while refusing to relinquish his liberalism. In his youth, he had been "a democrat but not the least of a socialist." But with time:

> We were now much less democrats than I had been, because as long as education continues to be so wretchedly imperfect, we dreaded the ignorance and especially the brutality of the mass; but our ideal of ultimate improvement went far beyond Democracy, and would class us decidedly under the general designation of Socialists.[44]

Democracy, he wrote in his *Autobiography*, "was no longer an absolute principle" worthy of defense. He wrote, in a spirit reminiscent of Plato, that "the best government (need it be said?) must be government of the wisest, and these must always be a few."[45]

Mill's socialist and anti-democratic streak only grew with age. His *Principles of Political Economy* tilted, with every few editions, increasingly away from free market principles toward a socialist conception of society. He argued that the distribution of goods is not indissolubly linked to their production, a claim which placed him squarely in opposition to one of the essential dogmas of all free market economics.

[40] Ibid., 175.
[41] Ibid., 168.
[42] Ibid., 178.
[43] Ibid., 174.
[44] Ibid., 238.
[45] John Stuart Mill, "On Democracy," *John Stuart Mill: A Selection of His Works* (New York: Odyssey Press, 1966), 456.

In economic matters, he frequently sought a middle way between laissez-faire and socialism. He defended inheritance taxes as a levy on an unearned windfall but argued against the progressive income tax as an unfair and unequal burden on higher earners. He accepted Locke's labor theory of property but like Marx, turned it to socialist purposes, arguing that landowners had no right to keep all of the unearned rents they received from their real property. He concluded that all foundations and philanthropic endowments "are national property, which the government may and ought to control."[46] In later editions of the *Principles*, he defended labor unions, farm cooperatives and even proposed the abolition of the wage system in favor of a cooperative wage system in which workers' earnings would be based on other workers' rankings of their productivity. His last major work, unfinished at his death, was a treatise working out the details of a decentralized, worker-centered socialism.[47]

In sum, Mill's view of history and political progress would have been broadly congenial to Marxists. And like Marx, Mill held in contempt the working class in existing society while nevertheless hoping (though with less certainty than Marx) that the selfishness of humanity was purely a product of the "merely provisional" social institutions that were destined to change. And though Mill decried the burgeoning totalitarian instinct which he recognized among the "reformers" to his left, his ideal society and the Marxian end-state were not that distinct from each other. Society has no authority over the individual, Mill wrote in his *Autobiography*, "except to enforce equal freedom of development for all individualities."[48] Here his usual skepticism toward government was blinkered for he apparently did not foresee the unfettered power this idea would bequeath to socialist governments in the twentieth century.

In the end, what made Mill a liberal was neither his faith in the common man nor a conviction that freedom requires less government. He had little of the former and was decidedly ambivalent about the latter. Rather, what made him a liberal was his faith in *progress* and his conviction that freedom as self-individuation best promotes it.

In a speech Mill gave during his campaign for Parliament, he cast the distinction between liberalism and conservatism in the pithiest of terms. "The liberal," he wrote, "is he who looks forward for his principles: the Tory looks backward for his." He concluded:

> I, therefore, think that both in politics and in other matters, there are truths which it is already time to proclaim, though in the existing state of opinion the time has not yet come when they can be carried into practice.… The only person

46 Mill, *Autobiography*, CW, 1:190.
47 John Stuart Mill, "Chapters on Socialism," in *Essays on Economics and Society*, CW, 5:703–53.
48 Mill, *Autobiography*, CW, 1:260.

> qualified to judge rightly or safely for today, is the one who includes tomorrow in his deliberations.[49]

It is clear from all this that Mill was no classical liberal or proto-libertarian. He called himself an "advanced liberal" and an "ideal socialist." Accordingly, the heart of his political thought falls much closer today to the libertarian socialism of Noam Chomsky than to the free market capitalism of Milton Friedman. Though he was more skeptical of paternalism and big government schemes than the modern progressive, his conception of *what freedom is* and his continuing attempts to harmonize liberty with equality, and freedom from government with freedom from society make him both the architect of modern progressive liberalism and the harbinger of other still more radical political creeds.

[49] Mill, *Speech of the Electors of Westminster*, 467–68. These words presage a more recent use of this idea. One can almost hear Fleetwood Mac's "Don't Stop Thinking about Tomorrow," as it was frequently played during Bill Clinton's presidential campaign of 1992.

PART II

Mill and the Constitution

4

Constitutional Liberties before Mill

This chapter is intended as an introduction to constitutional history for those readers who are not lawyers, though it may also serve as a review for those who are. It seeks to explain the evolution of our current understanding of constitutional rights and to place our constitutional tradition in the broader framework of the liberal tradition.

Let us begin by simply juxtaposing some important milestones, philosophically and constitutionally. As we have seen, the liberal tradition originated in the late seventeenth century with the natural rights/classical liberal philosophy of John Locke. Recall that Locke died in 1704, seventy years before the American Revolution. The Constitution was ratified in 1788 and the Bill of Rights, which included various protections for our individual liberties, three years later, on December 15, 1791. John Stuart Mill was born in 1806, three years after the Supreme Court's seminal decision, *Marbury* v. *Madison*.[1] It was in *Marbury* that the Court first firmly asserted its power of judicial review – the power on which the enforcement of all constitutional rights depends.

Yet, for reasons we will discuss, the Supreme Court was simply not much in the business of enforcing individual rights protected by the Constitution until the early twentieth century. It was not until 1905 that it began reading specifically Lockean values into our constitutional rights tradition in *Lochner* v. *New York*.[2] For the next three decades, the Supreme Court used the Due Process clause – a constitutional provision that has been the subject of more controversy than perhaps any other single provision – to protect a right to what the Court called "freedom of contract," a right they found central to the Anglo-American tradition of liberty stretching back to Locke and ultimately to the Magna Carta.[3] In sum, roughly two centuries separate the inception of classical liberal political thought from the Lochner era of classical liberal constitutionalism.

[1] 5 US 137 (1803).
[2] 198 US 45 (1905).
[3] *Lochner* v. *New York*, 198 US 45 (1905).

Similarly, while Mill published *On Liberty* in 1859, it took more than a century for his ideas and, indeed, his very conception of liberty, to find their way into the constitutional jurisprudence of the Supreme Court of the 1960s and beyond. The right to privacy, which partially realized Mill's "harm principle," was first recognized in *Griswold* v. *Connecticut* in 1965[4] and subsequently developed in cases such as *Roe* v. *Wade*, recognizing a right to abortion under the privacy right[5] and *Lawrence* v. *Texas*,[6] recognizing a privacy protecting consensual homosexual acts between adults. The greatly broadened protections for freedom of speech culminating in such cases as *Brandenburg* v. *Ohio*[7] in 1969 also reflect Mill's influence, as does the equal protection jurisprudence in the context of gender a decade or two later. Yet Mill's influence has, if anything, deepened with time – even as those whom he has influenced have largely forgotten his name. *Obergefeld* v. *Hodges*, the 2015 case recognizing a constitutional right to gay marriage is a direct legacy of Mill's influence – a fact openly acknowledged by the dissent.

Indeed, it is not an exaggeration to suggest that Mill's influence on American constitutionalism is far broader and deeper than Locke's influence was in the era preceding this. It is perhaps all the more ironic that many contemporary judges are, at best, only vaguely aware of the name, John Stuart Mill, or his influence on our constitutional tradition.

THE REPUBLICAN CONSTITUTION

Constitutional scholars frequently distinguish among three periods of American constitutionalism. We will refer to these as the "republican," the "classical liberal" and the "modern liberal" constitutional eras, respectively. So distinctive are these three eras in their differing understandings of federalism, democracy and the nature of individual rights that one prominent scholar refers to these as three distinct "republics."[8] Whether or not this is an exaggeration, it is certainly true that the American constitutional tradition has evolved through these three different periods in which our collective understanding of politics, the role of government and the nature of liberty itself have changed dramatically.

The first "republican" era of American constitutionalism runs from the ratification of the Constitution in 1788 to roughly 1868, when the Fourteenth Amendment was adopted. In a general sense, republican forms of government are those that are thought to advance what Isaiah Berlin called "positive liberty" and what Benjamin Constant referred to as

4 381 US 479 (1965).
5 410 US 113 (1973).
6 539 US 558 (2003).
7 395 US 444 (1969).
8 Bruce Ackerman, *We the People: Foundations* (Cambridge: Harvard University Press, 1998), 58–80.

"the liberty of the ancients."[9] Positive liberty is the liberty of the citizen to participate in government, to deliberate, to vote and to take part in various ways in governmental decision-making (i.e., jury service). This conception of liberty was perhaps most highly realized in ancient Athenian democracy – ergo, "the liberty of the ancients." It is positive liberty in the sense that the ideal of liberty is bound up with self-government, with law-making and with the active life of the citizen who participates fully in the democratic process. In its most idealized form, republicanism views the life of active participation by citizens in the *polis* as the highest form of human self-realization.[10]

In contrast to the republican ideal, liberalism values the undisturbed life of the individual outside of the public sphere. Liberty is connected to the values of individualism, autonomy and privacy. Liberal conceptions of freedom are "negative" in the sense that they involve non-interference by legal authorities, the absence of government control – a sphere in which the individual is free *from* government. Where republican liberty is the freedom to take part in the affairs of state, the liberal conception is captured by Justice Brandeis' notion of "a right to be let alone."[11]

Mill had written of the purer republican idea of freedom in *On Liberty*, casting it as the antecedent of more developed liberal ideas. The essence of this was that "the rulers should be identified with the people, that their interests and will should be the interests and will of the nation. The nation did not need to be protected against its own will."[12] But, with time, the republican idea was found to be wanting:

> The people who exercise the power are not always the same people with those over whom it is exercised; and the "self-government" spoken of is not the government of each by himself, but of each by all the rest. The will of the people, moreover, practically means the will of the most numerous or the most active part of the people … the tyranny of the majority is now generally included among the evils against which society requires to be on guard.[13]

[9] Isaiah Berlin, "Two Concepts of Liberty," in *Four Essays on Liberty* (Oxford: Oxford University Press, 1969); Benjamin Constant, *Political Writings* (Cambridge: Cambridge Texts in the History of Political Thought, 1988), 102–15. Berlin argued that negative liberty concerns the question "What is the area in which the subject – a person or group of persons – is or should be left to do or be what he is able to do or be without interference by other people" whereas positive liberty concerns "What, or who, is the source of control or interference that can determine someone to do, or be, this rather than that." Berlin, "Two Concepts of Liberty," at 121–22.

[10] See Quentin Skinner, *Liberty before Liberalism* (Cambridge: Cambridge University Press, 1998) (for an excellent description of the ideal); Hanna Arendt, *The Human Condition* (Chicago: Chicago University Press, 1958) (for an idealized modern conception); Benjamin R. Barber, *Strong Democracy* (Berkeley: University of California, 1984) (for a discussion of the democratic-republican ideal in a modern context).

[11] *Olmstead* v. *United States*, 277 US 438 (Brandeis, J., dissenting).

[12] John Stuart Mill, *On Liberty*, CW, 18:218.

[13] Ibid., 219.

Mill may have been thinking about the kind of place Rousseau had envisioned in his Social Contract but in the American experience, republican ideas were intermingled with liberal notions. At any rate, the first period of American constitutionalism was the most "republican" of the three eras in the sense that the constitutional arrangements reflected highly decentralized political power with a heavy emphasis on state and local democracy as the locus of individual freedom.

Political power under the Constitution was decentralized in several ways. First, it was broken up vertically between the federal government and the states. Criminal law, business law, tort and contract law, property, trust and probate law and family law, etc. were almost wholly matters of state law. Federal power was supreme in its own sphere under the Supremacy clause of Article VI, but highly circumscribed, limited largely to the enumerated powers of Article I, section 8. These powers included the right to tax, spend, raise an army, coin money, create a post office and the sleeping giant, the "commerce clause" of Article I, section 8, clause 3. The commerce clause gave Congress the power to regulate commerce "with foreign nations, among the several states and with the Indian tribes."[14] While this would be reinterpreted to give Congress almost unlimited power beginning in the 1940s, during the republican era it was interpreted narrowly to give Congress only the power to pass laws that were international in scope – to coordinate with foreign governments and the Indian tribes, which were legally autonomous, and to coordinate activities *among* – but *not within* – the states.

Second, federalism meant that power was broken up horizontally among the states, each of which was autonomous within its own sphere. States were free to experiment with different policies and laws, or simply to reflect the mores and lifestyle of its citizens. Justice Brandeis later referred to this as "the laboratory of the states" idea. Third, power was further distilled within state and federal governments by the separation of powers into the three branches – legislative, executive and judicial – along with the checks and balances between them. For example, the President could veto an act of Congress. Furthermore, treaties and the appointment of judges require the joint action of the President and the Senate. Fourth, at the federal level there were different constituencies for members of the House of Representatives (by district), for Senators (by state) and for President (the entire nation). These served the function Madison mentioned in *Federalist* 10, to "refine and enlarge" the passions and interests of local factions. Fifth, of course, there was the as-yet underdeveloped power of judicial review – the power of the courts to set aside laws that had been passed by the elected branches.

[14] US Const. Art. I, sec. 8, cl. 3.

During the republic era, democracy itself was kept "closer to the ground" in the sense that the ratio of US representatives to constituents was much lower than it is today. The very first US census, in 1790, revealed that there were then just under four million inhabitants in the United States. With a total of sixty-seven representatives in the House, the constituent-to-representative ratio was roughly one US representative for every 60,000 inhabitants. (Today, with 325 million inhabitants in the United States and a total membership in the House of 435, the ratio is just under one in 750,000.) And the ratio of constituents to state representatives averaged well below one in ten thousand at the state level. In sum, the average citizen then had far more direct control and contact with his representatives than we do today.

Liberty was thus cashed out largely in "positive" terms, a function of the citizens' level of input into democracy. The "negative" protections of constitutional rights, on the other hand, were almost unknown – particularly at the federal level. The Bill of Rights, of course, theoretically carved out protection for a host of important liberties: The First Amendment prohibited government from establishing a religion and protected the rights of free exercise of religion, speech, press and assembly, along with the right to petition the government. The Second Amendment protects "the right of the people to keep and bear arms." The Third Amendment (which has not had any use in recent history) prohibits government from quartering soldiers in homes during times of peace. The Fourth Amendment prohibits warrantless "searches and seizures" of "persons, houses, papers and effects." The Fifth Amendment includes several important measures including the double jeopardy clause, a right against self-incrimination in criminal cases, the right to a grand jury, the "takings" clause (prohibiting government from taking private property without just compensation) and the Due Process clause (prohibiting government from taking "life, liberty or property without due process of law"). The Sixth Amendment contains several important rights attendant to arrest, including the right to a jury trial, the right to retain counsel and the right to confront witnesses against the accused. The Seventh Amendment ensures the right to jury trial in civil cases. The Eighth Amendment protects against excessive bail and fines and prohibits the use of "cruel and unusual punishment."

The liberties protected in these eight amendments might serve as the bulwark of a genuinely liberal ideal of government – but they were of little avail during the first, republican, era of American constitutionalism. For one thing, the Bill of Rights applied only against *federal* power.[15] It did not apply to the states at all. Why was this? What could account for what appears to us today such an egregious gap in our constitutional protections?

[15] This understanding of the limits of the Bill of Rights was ratified in *Barron* v. *Baltimore*, 32 US 243 (1833), in which the Supreme Court held that the "takings" clause of the Fifth Amendment did not apply against the mayor of Baltimore when he authorized the diversion of waterways which affected the plaintiff's business. Its broader implication is that the Bill of Rights did not apply against state or municipal authorities.

The answer is that the Framers were not liberals; their conception of government was still broadly republican – as was their idea of liberty. While scholars over the last half-century have debated the extent to which the American founding was a "republican" or a "liberal" affair,[16] there can be little doubt that the Framers' conception of freedom was, in part, a *corporate* idea: the freedom of the individual depended on the freedom of the state. The essence of freedom was popular sovereignty and the opposite of freedom was not the violation of individual rights; it was *tyranny*.[17] Tyranny was least likely to occur where government was "closest to the People." Conversely, it was most likely to develop where it was far away and highly centralized (i.e., in the national government). Thus, those who favored a Bill or Rights – and many, including Madison, did not[18] – viewed it as a check only on federal power.

Not only was the national government the likely threat to liberty, as the Framers saw it, it generally lacked the authority to intrude into state affairs at any rate. The relationship between the national government and the states was not viewed to be one of subordination: the states were viewed, in most respects, as semi-autonomous sovereignties. State governments could take care of their own citizens – and, of course, state constitutions sometimes provided for many of the same liberties against state power, though there were differences and gaps in coverage. But it was simply not the federal government's business to protect the individual from his own state. They neither had the power nor the right to do so. This would all change with the adoption of the Fourteenth Amendment in 1868.

Even where the Bill of Rights applied as a protection against federal power, some thought its effect was only advisory. No less an authority that John Marshall, who later authored *Marbury* v. *Madison*, declared in the Virginia ratifying convention in 1788 that while the Courts could declare federal laws unconstitutional under the structural provisions of the Constitution – under separation of powers principles or where Congress exceeded its power, for example – the Bill of Rights created only "recommendatory" limits on federal power. They were intended to provide moral *guidance* to Congress but were not strict limits on the ultimate exercise of its power.

[16] For a "republican" take on the founding, see Gordon S. Wood, *The Creation of the American Republic, 1776–1787* (Chapel Hill: University of North Carolina, 1998); Bernard Bailyn, *The Ideological Origins of the American Revolution* (Cambridge: Belknap Press of Harvard University Press, 1992); Thomas R. Pangle, *The Spirit of Modern Republicanism* (Chicago: University of Chicago Press, 1988). For a critique of these, see Joyce Appleby, "Republicanism and Ideology," 37 *American Quarterly* 461 (1985).

[17] John Phillip Reid, *The Concept of Liberty in the Age of the American Revolution* (Chicago: University of Chicago Press, 1988).

[18] Madison came around to accepting the addition of a Bill of Rights as long as it was clear, he argued, that its inclusion was not intended to imply that these new rights would be construed to broaden federal power, that is, as long as a Ninth and Tenth Amendment were included to make clear that the enumeration of rights was not intended to imply that the federal government could exceed its powers as long as it did not violate rights. See David N. Mayer, *The Constitutional Thought of Thomas Jefferson* (Charlottesville: University Press of Virginia, 1992), 150–55 (for a good discussion of Jefferson and Madison's positions on the Bill of Rights).

"Otherwise," Marshall opined, "many laws which would be convenient would be unconstitutional."[19]

We also have to remember finally that even where the Supreme Court technically had the power to act, it was still generally jealous of its limited institutional authority relative to the other branches. For good reason Hamilton had called the courts "the least dangerous branch" in *Federalist* 78: Congress held the power of the purse and the President was commander-in-chief of the army and navy, but the Court held no real power over the other branches. What could it do if the other branches simply ignored its rulings? The Court's sense of institutional weakness underscores the irony of *Marbury* v. *Madison*, the 1803 case remembered today for the Court's confident assertion of the power of judicial review. Yet it was anything but this.

President John Adams, a Federalist, and the Federalist Congress were swept out of office by Jefferson and the Democratic-Republicans in the election of 1800. On their last day in office, the Federalists created forty-two justice of the peace commissions for Marbury and other federalists, but Marbury's commission was never delivered. When Marbury requested that his commission be delivered, Madison, Jefferson's new Secretary of State, refused to hand it over. Marbury then brought suit, asking the Federalist-dominated Supreme Court to award him his commission. But rather than ordering Madison to turn over the commission – an order the Court knew Madison would ignore – it held unconstitutional the provision of the Judiciary Act of 1789 under which Marbury brought suit. The upshot of this enigmatic ruling is that the Court asserted its power of judicial review to hold that it lacked the power to grant fellow-Federalist Marbury his commission. Thus, the Court claimed the right of judicial review, in part, to avoid the embarrassment of having a contrary order ignored.

The only Supreme Court cases recognizable to us today as individual rights cases during this period were a few cases decided under the "Contracts clause" of Article I, section 10 of the Constitution. Article I, section 10 was the only rights-like section in the original Constitution that explicitly applied to the states.[20] Among the various provisions of this section was the Contracts clause, which prohibits states from "impairing the Obligation of Contracts."[21] While there is debate about whether this

[19] Edward S. Corbin, *Liberty against Government* (Baton Rouge: Louisiana State University Press, 1948), 59.

[20] States were prohibited from passing ex post facto laws and Bills of Attainder and, though they function as immunities from state power, these clauses do not single out particular kinds of activities for protection. The Contracts clause is "rights-like" in a way that these other provisions are not in the sense that it protects a particular kind of activity (e.g., speech, press, freedom of religion) such as the right to contract, as here.

[21] Article I, section 10, clause 1 reads: "No State shall enter into any Treaty, Alliance or Confederation; grant letters of Marque and Reprisal; coin Money; emit Bills of Credit; make any Thing but gold and silver Coin a Tender in Payment of Debts; pass any Bill of Attainder, ex post facto Law or Law impairing the Obligation of Contracts, or grant any Title of Nobility."

clause was intended simply to prevent popular majorities in the states from passing legislation to cancel previously existing debts, or more generally to have the anti-regulatory function the Due Process clause would later have in the Lochner era, the Supreme Court and lower courts did use the clause with some frequency during the first period of American constitutional law.[22]

There were also a few splashy endorsements of the classical liberal/natural law idea, but they never had any real legal effect. The most famous of these was *Calder* v. *Bull*, decided in 1798.[23] The Connecticut legislature voted to reverse a will in which Calder had an interest, transferring that interest to Bull. Since the Connecticut constitution did not at that time have a bill of rights, state law afforded Calder no remedy. He sued under the federal Constitution claiming that the legislative act violated the ex post facto laws under Article I, section 10 of the federal Constitution. The justices determined that the *ex post facto* clause limited only criminal laws, not civil. But Justice Samuel Chase argued that natural law principles should be used to set aside the unjust result:

> There are acts which the federal or state legislatures cannot do without exceeding their authority. … An act of the legislature (for I cannot call it a law) contrary to the great principles of the social compact cannot be considered a rightful exercise of legislative authority. … A law that punishes an innocent action … a law that destroys, or impairs, the lawful private contracts of citizens, a law that makes a man a judge in his own case, or a law that takes property from A and gives it to B; it is against all reason and justice for a people to entrust a legislature with such powers, and therefore it cannot be presumed that they have done it. The genius, the nature and the spirit of our state governments amount to a prohibition against such acts legislation; and general principles of law and reason forbid them.[24]

Lofty rhetoric, this – yet Justice Chase was alone in the vote and *Calder* v. *Bull* has no precedential value except insofar as it held that the *ex post facto* clause provides no protection in a case such as this.

There was only one case during this entire era when the Supreme Court used a provision of the Bill of Rights to protect a constitutional right – and this one was a disaster. This was the infamous *Dred Scott* case decided in 1857. To call this case an "individual rights" case is a supreme irony but is was, in fact, the only case from this first era in which the Supreme Court invoked a provision of the Bill of Rights to limit federal power. Scott was a slave who had been taken, by his owner, to free territory in what is now Minnesota. Scott attempted to claim that this change in location rendered him free – that is, that by going to a "free" territory, he was now legally

[22] *Fletcher* v. *Peck*, 10 US 87 (1810) was the first of these – and the first case in which the Supreme Court held a state law unconstitutional.
[23] 3 US (3 Dall) 386 (1798).
[24] 3 US at 389.

free. But Chief Justice Taney, a southerner and slave-owner himself, ruled that the Due Process clause of the Fifth Amendment protected the slaveholder's right to the "property" he had in his slaves.[25] To do this, the Court had to hold unconstitutional the Missouri Compromise of 1820, the federal act that rendered this territory "free" and that required that new states had to be added to the Union two at a time – one Free and one Slave.

By ensuring that neither side could command a majority in the Senate, the Missouri Compromise had maintained the precarious political balance between Slave and Free states. The ruling, in effect, permitted slaveholders to bring slaves to "free" areas administered under federal law without fear of forfeiting the property interests they claimed in their slaves.

In sum, the first individual rights case decided under the Bill of Rights by the Supreme Court was the greatest anti-individual rights case of all time. Moreover, by upsetting the tenuous political balance between Free and Slave states, the *Dred Scott* case helped pave the way to the Civil War.[26]

THE BIRTH OF THE CLASSICAL LIBERAL CONSTITUTION

After the Civil War ended in 1865, three constitutional amendments were passed in quick succession. The Thirteenth Amendment, ratified on December 31, 1865, abolished "involuntary servitude" in the United States. This is the only provision of the Constitution which has been interpreted to apply to individual citizens. All other constitutional provisions constrain only the government, not private parties.[27] The Fourteenth Amendment, which included the Due Process and Equal Protection clauses, was ratified in 1868, and the Fifteenth, which recognizes a right to vote for African-American men, became law in 1870.[28]

Of the three new amendments, the Fourteenth worked the most far-reaching changes in the American constitutional order. Section 1 of the Fourteenth Amendment provides:

> All persons born or naturalized in the United States, and subject to the jurisdiction thereof, are citizens of the United States and of the State wherein they reside. No

[25] The Due Process clause of the Fifth Amendment provides "No person shall be … deprived of life, liberty, or property, without due process of law."

[26] The Dred Scott opinion held unconstitutional the Missouri Compromise of 1820, the federal act by which new states were added to the Union two at a time, one Free and the other Slave. This ensured against the possibility that one or the other side would achieve a majority in the Senate, permitting them to extend or abolish slavery.

[27] The Constitution protects all persons from infringements by government, not other individuals. Constitutional right protections thus apply only as against government. Protections from what other individuals may do – for example, where an individual discriminates on the basis of race, or prevents another person from speaking or voting – come from our various civil rights statutes.

[28] The Fifteenth Amendment provides, in relevant part, that a person may not be denied the right to vote "on the basis of race, color, or previous condition of servitude." US Constitution, Amend. XV.

> State shall make or enforce any law which shall abridge the privileges or immunities of citizens of the United States; nor shall any State deprive any person of life, liberty, or property, without due process of law; nor deny to any person within its jurisdiction the equal protection of the laws.

The first clause recognizes the citizenship of all persons born or naturalized in the United States. This was written to overrule that portion of the *Dred Scott* ruling which held that all African-Americans, free and slave alike, were not – and had never been intended to be – United States citizens under the Constitution.[29] The following three clauses of section 1 prohibited the states from passing or enforcing any law that "abridge the privileges or immunities" of any US citizen (the "Privileges or Immunities" clause), or that "deprives any person of life, liberty or property without due process of law" (the Due Process clause) or that denies to any person within its jurisdiction "the equal protection of the laws" (the Equal Protection clause).

The meaning and scope of each of the three clauses was not immediately clear: What was included among the protected "privileges and immunities"? What process was *due*, exactly, concerning the protection of life, liberty and property? And how broadly should the equal protection clause be interpreted? More generally, the question was whether the Fourteenth Amendment was intended chiefly to protect the newly freed slaves and free blacks living in the North, or whether it had a much broader and constitutionally significant function – to nationalize the protection of civil liberties for all.

Those in Congress who debated the Fourteenth Amendment clearly saw the dilemma. The problem with the broader position was that it amounted, as several congressman pointed out, to a radical transfer of power from the state to the federal government. That such a transfer was intended was supported by section 5 of the Fourteenth Amendment, which created a new federal power – that "Congress shall have power to enforce, by appropriate legislation, the provisions of this article." But those on the other side pointed out that the motivating reason for the Fourteenth Amendment was to protect the newly freed slaves, not to achieve some broader and far more radical constitutional aim.

The Supreme Court's first attempt to answer these questions occurred five years after the adoption of the Fourteenth Amendment, in 1873, in the so-called *Slaughterhouse Cases*.[30] This was, by chance, the same year Mill died.

29 "The question before us is whether the class of persons described in the plea in abatement compose a portion of the people, and are a constituent portion of this sovereignty? We think they are not, and that they are not included, and were not intended to be included, under the word 'citizen' in the Constitution, and can therefore claim none of the rights and privileges which that instrument provides for and secures to citizens of the United States. *Dred Scott* v. *Sandford*, 60 US at 393. Section 1 of the Fourteenth Amendment overrules this holding and provides that all persons "born or naturalized in the United States are citizens thereof."

30 *Slaughterhouse Cases*, 83 US 36 (1873).

The *Slaughterhouse Cases* arose as the result of a cholera epidemic caused when roughly a thousand butchers working upstream from New Orleans deposited animal offal and other remains into waterways that fed the city. The state responded by permitting New Orleans to charter a municipal corporation that centralized all butchering operations in one area outside the city limits. Butchers were required to move their operations to this site and to pay a fee to the corporation to rent a place to practice their trade. Butchers brought suit under all three clauses of section 1 claiming, among other things, that the law denied them their basic "privilege and immunities" to work where they wished, that it violated their property interests under the Due Process clause and that it discriminated between butchers and other occupations in violation of the Equal Protection clause. In sum, the case had nothing specifically to do with race.

A narrowly divided Court decided, on a 5–4 vote, for the narrower and less radical interpretation, rejecting the butchers' arguments. Justice Miller, who wrote the majority opinion, concluded that the petitioners' arguments would make the Supreme Court "a perpetual censor" on state legislation. The majority upheld the corporate charter determining, in essence, that the three new clauses of the Constitution had no effect in a case such as this. Miller opined that, "we doubt very much whether any action of a state not directed by way of discrimination against the negroes as a class, or on account of their race, will ever be held to come within the purview of… the Equal Protection clause."[31]

The Due Process and Equal Protection clauses have since been rehabilitated, as we will see, but the Court's treatment of the Privileges or Immunities clause gave it a very narrow construction – indeed, a construction that rendered the clause a virtual nullity.[32] Most scholars today agree that the clause was intended to extend constitutional protection for the liberties protected by the Bill of Rights (and perhaps other liberties not enumerated) to the states. Yet the Court rejected this interpretation precisely because it was so contrary to the republican model of government that had prevailed from the time of the framing of the Constitution. The butchers' interpretation of the clause could not be correct, the Court stated, because it "radically changes the relation of the State and Federal governments, and of both these governments to the People.… We are convinced that no such results were intended by Congress."[33] Protection of individual rights from state law "must rest for their security and protection where they have hitherto rested" – with the states.

[31] 83 US at 81.

[32] The Court limited the clause to the protection of certain *federal* privileges and immunities which were already protected under the privileges and immunities clause of the original Constitution, Article IV, Section 2. That clause provides that "the citizens of each state shall be entitled to all privileges and immunities of citizens in the several states." In other words, states could not limit the federal privileges and immunities of all citizens of the United States. The *Slaughterhouse* opinion treated the Fourteenth Amendment's version of the clause as a replica of the earlier clause.

[33] 83 US at 78–79.

But, then, what were the "privileges" and "immunities" which this clause of the Fourteenth Amendment was intended to protect? Justice Miller responded wanly that "it would be more tedious than difficult to enumerate" what these rights are. The rights protected by the clause were essentially, according to the Court, the old positive liberties: "to come to the seat of government to assert any claim he may have…, to transact any business he may have with it, to seek its protection, to share its offices, to engage in administering its functions."[34] These were liberties which, as Miller himself noted, were already protected under the original Constitution.

Philosophically, the *Slaughterhouse* decision clung to the older republican view of liberty. Constitutionally, it left the Privileges or Immunities clause of the Fourteenth Amendment a redundancy at best and a dead letter at worst. While there have been occasional attempts to restore it to its rightful place in modern constitutional law, these have not been successful.[35]

But from the ashes of the Privileges or Immunities clause arose the phoenix of the classical liberal interpretation of constitutional rights. In two dissents in the *Slaughterhouse* cases, Justices Field and Bradley began to make the case that the Fourteenth Amendment was intended to nationalize the protection of civil liberties and that these liberties were closely connected to the right to property and the right to labor. Justice Field put it boldly: the Privileges or Immunities clause "was intended to give practical effect to the Declaration of Independence of 1776 of inalienable rights, rights which are the gift of the Creator, which the law does not confer, but only recognizes."[36] The nature of this right was:

> the right to pursue a lawful employment in a lawful manner, without other restraint than such as equally affects all persons… Everywhere, all pursuits, all professions, all avocations are open without restrictions except for those that are imposed equally on all.[37]

While Field did not appeal to Locke, he did quote Adam Smith to the effect that the most "sacred and inviolable right" is the "property which each man has in his own labor."[38] Any regulation which interferes with economic relationships "hinders the one from working at what he thinks proper, and [and] hinders the others from employing whom they think proper."[39]

Justice Bradley appealed to the Anglo-American tradition of freedom which, in his words, embodied "the rights of Englishmen: the rights which had been wrested

[34] Ibid., at 79.

[35] Most recently, Justice Thomas urged the Court to restore the clause to its rightful constitutional place in his concurrence in *MacDonald* v. *City of Chicago*, 561 US 742, 806 (2010) – the case that incorporated the Second Amendment against the states.

[36] 83 US at 115–16 (Field, J., dissenting).

[37] Ibid., at 110.

[38] Adam Smith, *Wealth of Nations*, bk. I, ch. 10, par. 2, quoted at 83 US 110 (Field, J., dissenting).

[39] Ibid., at 110.

from English sovereigns at various points in the nation's history."[40] These were negative rights, and they were bound up with economic liberties. What is even more significant about his opinion is his view of the clause that supports these rights: Reacting to the Court's nullification of the Privileges or Immunities clause, or perhaps, anticipating what was to happen in the twentieth century, Justice Bradley transferred the weight of the protection of these basic liberties to the Due Process clause: "Life, liberty and property are forbidden to be taken without due process of law."[41]

While the Framers of the original Constitution were not strangers to these classical liberal values – the Fifth Amendment's proscription against taking "life, liberty or property without due process of law" and the Contract clause's protection of vested contractual interests attest to this – what had changed was the realization that the old republican institutions grounded on popular sovereignty were not enough to protect these rights. Individual rights needed the protection of the courts. Standardizing these rights across the states required the centripetal influence of the federal judiciary, and the Supreme Court in particular.

It was at this moment in history that a Michigan Supreme Court justice and future Dean of the University of Michigan Law School, Thomas Cooley, published the most influential work of constitutional theory in the late nineteenth century. Cooley's *Constitutional Limitations* appeared in 1868, the same year the Fourteenth Amendment was adopted. Cooley was a committed classical liberal, but not a natural rights theorist. His classical liberalism was of the nineteenth-century strain, influenced by Bentham and Austin, rather than Locke and Justice Chase of *Calder* v. *Bull*. Government power had to be limited not by invocation of un-enumerated constitutional rights, but by strict construction of government power.[42] Cooley argued that the "police power" of the state was limited to the protection of health, safety and morals – bases for power which precluded paternalistic and redistributionist tendencies of socialists, progressives and others. Cooley's treatise was the dominant statement of constitutional theory at the time when the future justices of the *Lochner* Court were law students or young lawyers.[43] Even Justice Louis Brandeis, who did not share the Lochnerian vision, was influenced by Cooley.[44]

In the wake of the *Slaughterhouse* cases, there were a series of opinions in the last quarter of the nineteenth century in which the Court slowly groped its way

[40] 83 US at 114 (Bradley, J., dissenting).

[41] Ibid., at 127.

[42] Thomas M. Cooley, *Constitutional Limitations* (Boston: Little, Brown and Company, 2nd ed., 1871), 163–69 and 174–76.

[43] Between 1888 and 1898, six new justices were added who had been raised on Cooley and like influences. Five of these would make up the Lochner Court. Corwin, *Liberty against Government*, at 146.

[44] One of Justice Brandeis's most remembered expressions uttered in the name of constitutional privacy, though in dissent, was that we have "a right to be let alone." This expression itself originated in Cooley's treatise.

toward the protection of economic liberties. Most of these cases upheld state legislation, but with warnings, in *dicta*, that there were limits to the police power of the states.[45] Indeed, in 1886, a second important constitutional treatise appeared with exactly this title and import. It was Christopher Tiedeman's, *A Treatise on the Limitations of the Police Power in the United States*, which was, if anything, even more strident in its opposition to collectivism, socialism and to labor movements, in particular.[46]

Finally, by 1897, now with a new majority steeped in the constitutional liberalism of Cooley and Tiedeman, the Court decided *Allgeyer* v. *Louisiana*, the first case in which the Court held that the Due Process clause protects economic liberties.[47] The Court unanimously held unconstitutional a Louisiana law which prohibited in-state persons or companies from insuring their property with out-of-state companies that had not registered with the state. While the Court here relied in part on the interstate effects of the law (i.e., states cannot pass laws burdening interstate commerce with businesses in other states), Justice Peckham wrote that the law violated the Due Process right of freedom of contract. He adopted Justice Bradley's reasoning from Bradley's *Slaughterhouse* dissent, stating:

> The "liberty" mentioned in [the Fourteenth] amendment means not only the right of the citizen to be free from the mere physical restraint of his person, as by incarceration, but the term is deemed to embrace the right of the citizen to be free in the enjoyment of all his faculties, to be free to use them in all lawful ways, to live and work where he will, to earn his livelihood by any lawful calling, to pursue any livelihood or avocation, and for that purpose *to enter into all contracts which may be proper, necessary, and essential* to his carrying out to a successful conclusion the purposes above mentioned.[48]

The *Lochner* case was still eight years in the future, but the Lochner era had begun.

45 In *Munn* v. *Illinois*, 94 US 113 (1877), for example, Illinois passed a law setting maximum prices for grain storage warehouses. The Court upheld the law, holding that the state has more power to regulate when private property is used in a way that is "affected with a public interest." But the Court warned that regulatory laws such as this might violate the Due Process clause "under certain circumstances." The extent to which regulation reduced the value of property was a matter of degree but, at some point, as the Court explained in *The Railroad Commission* cases, 116 US 307 (1886), the state could go too far. The Court here upheld fare and freight regulations with a similar warning that the "power to regulate is not a power to destroy." In *Mugler* v. *Kansas*, 123 US 623 (1887), the petitioner had built a beer brewery in 1877. The state subsequently passed a prohibition law and Mugler was found guilty of manufacturing and selling beer. The Court rejected his challenge under the Due Process and "Takings" clauses, holding that the statute fell within the 'health, safety and morals' ambit of the state's police power. Justice Field dissented.

46 Christopher G. Tiedeman, *A Treatise on the Limitations of the Police Power in the United States* (St. Louis: F. H. Thomas Law Book, 1886).

47 *Allgeyer* v. *Louisiana*, 165 US 578 (1897).

48 165 US at 589.

FROM LOCKE TO *LOCHNER*: THE CLASSICAL LIBERAL CONCEPTION OF CONSTITUTIONAL RIGHTS

In 1905, the Court decided *Lochner* v. *New York*.[49] New York had passed a law prohibiting workers from working more than ten hours a day and sixty hours a week.[50] The state had argued that this fell squarely within the police power of the state; that is, that the law protected bakers from various pulmonary conditions caused by breathing the granulated dust over excessive periods of time and that it protected the health of the general public by preventing contagious diseases that might flow either from the poor health or the unsanitary work habits of exhausted bakers. But the Court rejected these arguments, concluding that the law "involves neither the safety, the morals nor the welfare of the public, and the interest of the public is not in the slightest degree affected by such as act."[51]

There were only two other possible justifications for the law – paternalistic and redistributive. But the Court dismissed the paternalistic implications of the law: "There is no contention that bakers as a class are not equal in intelligence and capacity to men in other trades.... They are in no sense wards of the State." At any rate, "there would seem to be no length to which legislation of this nature might not go."[52] The Court made only the briefest reference to what it guessed was the real motive of the law – that it was passed by a progressive legislature in a period of expanding government power to protect bakers' unions from competition at the expense of smaller, family-owned bakeries with fewer employees who worked longer hours.[53]

The Court held the law unconstitutional, stating that "the right to purchase or to sell labor is part of the liberty protected by the [fourteenth] amendment." In this case, the "statute necessarily interferes with the right to contract between the employer and employees concerning the number of hours in which the latter may labor."[54]

The case was decided narrowly, by a 5–4 margin, and Justice Holmes was among the dissenters:

> This case is decided upon an economic theory, which a large part of the country does not entertain. If it were a question whether I agreed with that theory, I should desire to study it further and long before making up my mind. But I do not conceive that to be my duty, because I strongly believe that my agreement or disagreement has nothing to do with the right of a majority to embody their opinions in law.[55]

[49] 198 US 45 (1905).
[50] 198 US at 52.
[51] *Lochner*, 198 US at 57.
[52] 198 US at 58.
[53] "It is impossible for us to shut our eyes to the fact that many of the laws of this character, while passed under what is claimed to be the police power for the purpose of protecting the public health or welfare are, in reality, passed from other motives... it seems to us that real object and purpose were to regulate the hours of labor between the master and the employee." 198 US at 63–64, Randy E. Barnett, *Our Republic Constitution* (New York: Harper-Collins, 2016), 138.
[54] Ibid., at 53.
[55] Ibid., at 75.

He went on, addressing the heart of the classical, and to some extent the Millian, idea of freedom:

> The liberty of the citizen to do as he likes so long as he does not interfere with the liberty of others to do the same, which has been a shibboleth for some well-known writers, is interfered with by school laws, by the Post Office, by every state or municipal institution which takes his money for purposes thought desirable, whether he likes it or not. The Fourteenth Amendment does not enact Mr. Herbert Spencer's Social Statics.[56]

Holmes was not alone in his skepticism of the doctrine later known to lawyers as "substantive due process." Progressives accused the Court of reading its own political and economic values into the Constitution. Teddy Roosevelt, who was President when *Lochner* was decided, regularly lambasted the "bakeshop case" as a version of conservative judicial activism and an incursion into the rights of the democratic majority.

For almost the next thirty years, the Supreme Court continued to use the Due Process clause to protect freedom of contract in a series of other cases. In one of the more far-reaching of cases, it invalidated a state law that sought to protect workers' rights for collective bargaining. In that case, *Coppage* v. *Kansas*,[57] Kansas passed a law that outlawed "yellow dog contracts" – contracts that required employees to relinquish their right to collective bargaining as a condition of employment. The Court ruled that such contracts, required as a condition of being hired, were part of the right to freedom of contract protected by Due Process. The Court acknowledged the disparity in bargaining power between employers and employees but observed, as classical liberals long had insisted, that

> where the right of private property exists, there must and will be inequalities of fortune [such that] it is impossible to uphold freedom of contract and the right of private property without at the same time recognizing those inequalities of fortune that are the necessary result of the exercise of those rights.[58]

In *Adkins* v. *Children's Hospital*, it struck down a District of Columbia minimum wage law.[59] And in a series of other cases, it struck down regulations on the price of gasoline[60] and other commodities.[61] The Court also invalidated licensing laws limiting entry into various professions.[62]

[56] Ibid.
[57] 236 US 1 (1915).
[58] Ibid., at 17.
[59] 261 US 525 (1923).
[60] *Williams* v. *Standard Oil Co.*, 278 US 235 (1929).
[61] *Ribnik* v. *McBride*, 277 US 350 (1928) (striking down a regulation of employment agency fees); *Tyson* v. *Brother & Banton*, 273 US 418 (1927) (regulations of theater tickets).
[62] *New State Ice Co.* v. *Lieberman*, 285 US 262 (1932) (invalidating requirement that ice dealers obtain certificate of convenience); *Louis K. Liggett Co.* v. *Baldridge*, 278 US 105 (1928) (invalidating a law that limited the business ownership of pharmacies to licensed pharmacists).

Yet the laissez-faire doctrine of the Lochner era was not monolithically enforced. The Court sometimes drew exceptions where it thought necessary. In 1898, a year after *Allgeyer*, the Court upheld a maximum hours law for miners.[63] Though *Lochner* came later, the *Lochner* Court made clear that *Hardy* was still good law, distinguishing mining from baking on the basis of the dangerousness of the mining profession. And just three years after *Lochner*, in *Muller* v. *Oregon*, the Court considered a sixty-hour working week limitation for women employed in various industries.[64] The future justice Brandeis, who argued the case for the state, wrote a one-hundred-page brief detailing the scientific evidence that long working hours were more dangerous to women than to men. The Court took judicial notice of the evidence and upheld the law.[65] In 1917, the Court upheld another Oregon law which limited to sixty hours a week, men and women's hours – exactly as the law in *Lochner* had. This latter case essentially overruled *sub silencio* the specific ruling of *Lochner*.

In two other cases, the Court made clear that the "liberty" protected by the Due Process clause was not limited to economic liberties. In these cases, decided in the 1920s, the Court extended the concept of liberty to include a right of family autonomy to educate children in a manner thought appropriate by their parents. In *Meyer* v. *Nebraska*,[66] the Court invalidated a Nebraska law that made it illegal to teach a foreign language in primary schools. The state had claimed that the purpose of the law was to promote civic virtue by ensuring that children learned English as their mother tongue but, passed in the wake of World War I, the law was probably intended to prohibit the teaching of German in the public schools.[67] The Court referenced Plato's plan to raise children collectively at birth, and Sparta's separation of parents and children at the age of seven:

> Although such measures have been deliberately approved by men of great genius, their ideas touching the relation between individual and State were wholly different from those upon which our institutions rest, and it hardly will be affirmed that any legislature could impose such restrictions upon the people of a State without doing violence to both letter and spirit of the Constitution.[68]

"Liberty," it said:

> denotes not merely freedom from bodily restraint, but also the right of the individual to contract, to engage in any of the common occupations of life, to acquire useful knowledge, to marry, establish a home and bring up children, to worship

[63] *Holden* v. *Hardy*, 169 US 366 (1898).
[64] 208 US 412 (1908).
[65] Alpheus T. Mason, *Brandeis: A Free Man's Life* (New York: The Viking Press, 1946), 248–54.
[66] 262 US 390 (1923).
[67] 262 US at 401.
[68] Ibid., at 402.

> God according to the dictates of his own conscience, and generally to enjoy those privileges long recognized at common law as essential to the orderly pursuit of happiness by free men.[69]

The second case, *Pierce* v. *Society of Sisters*, was decided two years later in 1925.[70] It held unconstitutional an Oregon statute which outlawed all private education, including religious education, requiring students to go to public schools. Where the law in *Meyer* had been motivated by anti-German prejudice, the law in *Pierce* was the result of anti-Catholic sentiments (though one of the affected plaintiffs was a private military academy). The Court again admonished the Oregon lawmakers who had passed the law that "the child is not the mere creature of the State" and reiterated the fundamental right of parents to raise and educate their children.[71]

These cases raise interesting questions about the relationship between the classical and the modern liberal conceptions of freedom in the personal sphere. Indeed, forty years later, Justice Douglas would quote approvingly the passage from *Meyer* to the effect that liberty included the right to "marry, establish a home and bring up children" in his opinion in *Griswold* v. *Connecticut*, the inaugural privacy right decision.[72] Yet, as various scholars have argued, these are two distinct rights based on two distinction conceptions of freedom: the modern liberal idea views this liberty as part of a quintessentially individual right of autonomy (i.e., to live one's life according to one's own plan) whereas the classical liberal idea was a right of *family* autonomy grounded on the moral and social importance of the nuclear family as the institution for child-rearing and as a bulwark against government power.[73]

THE DEMISE OF *LOCHNER* AND THE RISE OF THE MODERN LIBERAL ERA

At another time in history, *Meyer* and *Pierce* might have represented a promising constitutional working out of a fuller conception of the classical ideal of liberty – one that embraced personal and familial liberties. But *Pierce* was decided just four years before the Stock Market crashed in October 1929. A new world dawned, and the Supreme Court would soon reconsider its freedom of contract jurisprudence. Franklin Delano Roosevelt took office in 1933 promising a "New Deal" and a social contract that was in stark conflict with the values of the *Lochner* Court. The mood of the country had clearly shifted. In an age of widespread economic insecurity, the Court was faced with an entirely new social and political reality. Various members of the Court took the election of 1932 as a signal of the shift in American politics and, as the cartoonist had written, "the Court follows the election returns."

69 Ibid., at 399.
70 268 US 510 (1925).
71 Ibid., at 535.
72 Griswold, 381 US at 488.
73 See, e.g. Michael J. Sandel, *Democracy's Discontent: America in Search of a Public Philosophy* (Cambridge, MA: Harvard University Press, 1996), 91–119.

Within a year of F.D.R.'s taking office, the Court decided *Nebbia* v. *New York*, upholding a New York law that regulated the price of milk.[74] *Nebbia* undercut several other Lochner-era decisions that struck down price regulations in various industries. The writing was on the wall – almost. But in two important commerce clause cases in 1935 and 1936, the Court struck down important provisions of Roosevelt's New Deal, arguing that Congress had exceeded its power under the commerce clause. While these decisions were not based on the Due Process clause, they were generally pert of the limited government jurisprudence of the era: they held the line on the expanding power of the federal government. Also in 1936 came the last decision consistent with the *Lochner* philosophy, a case that applied the ban on minimum wage laws to the states.[75]

From 1934 to 1937, the direction of the Court's majority seemed to hang in the balance. After his resounding reelection in 1936, Roosevelt assumed that he now had the mandate from the voters to take more affirmative measures where the Supreme Court was involved. He threatened to "pack the Court" with six new progressive-minded justices – for a total of fifteen – to shift the Court's center of gravity to the Left. This, of course, would have had disastrous consequences for the institutional integrity of the Supreme Court. Legend has it that Justice Owen Roberts, one of the swing-vote justices, changed his vote to the liberal side – just in time – in *West Coast Hotel* v. *Parrish*. A journalist later parodied this as "the switch in time that saved nine." In fact, Roberts had not switched his vote at all. He accepted Roosevelt's reelection as an indication of the popularity, if not the necessity, of his New Deal programs.

That case, *West Coast Hotel* v. *Parrish*, upheld a state minimum wage law.[76] The case not only overruled *Adkins* v. *Children's Hospital*, decided just fourteen years earlier, it radically inverted the concept of liberty protected by the Due Process clause:

> The constitutional provision invoked is the due process clause of the Fourteenth Amendment governing the states, as the due process clause invoked in the Adkins case governed Congress. In each case, the violation alleged by those attacking minimum wage regulation for women is deprivation of freedom of contract. What is this freedom? The Constitution does not speak of freedom of contract. It speaks of liberty and prohibits the deprivation of liberty without due process of law. In prohibiting that deprivation, the Constitution does not recognize an absolute and uncontrollable liberty. Liberty in each of its phases has its history and connotation. But the liberty safeguarded is liberty in a social organization which requires the protection of law against the evils which menace the health, safety, morals, and welfare of the people. Liberty under the Constitution is thus *necessarily subject to the restraints of due process*, and regulation which is reasonable in relation to its subject and is adopted in the interests of the community is due process.[77]

[74] 291 US 502 (1934).
[75] *Morehead* v. *New York ex rel. Tipaldo*, 298 US 587 (1936).
[76] 300 US 379 (1937).
[77] 300 US at 391 (my italics).

The Court seemed to be saying here that the Due Process clause was no longer a check on government but rather the measure of a just balance between individual liberty and social legislation. Indeed, in saying that "the liberty safeguarded is liberty in a social organization which requires the protection of law," the Court was indicating that legislation can further liberty – that law is not always an invasion of liberty but can instead promote liberty by seeking a just balance of social interests and individual rights. In sum, the Court was moving toward a more positive conception of rights – one that views law not as a limit to liberty, but as a means for enhancing it.

Two weeks later, in its *National Labor Relations Board* v. *Jones and Laughlin Steel*, the Court capitulated on the commerce clause issue, acknowledging for the first time in history sweeping congressional powers under the commerce clause.[78] Thus, the demise of *Lochner* came hand-in-hand with this exponential expansion of federal power in economic matters.

A new era was dawning. Already by 1943, the Court began to unfold a far more novel and recent conception of liberty. In *West Virginia State Board of Education* v. *Barnette*, the Court held for the first time that the individual's liberty of conscience, protected by the First Amendment, prohibited government from compelling the individual to recite the Pledge of Allegiance.[79] In that opinion, Justice Jackson, one of F.D.R's newest appointees, offered both a post-mortem on *Lochner* and a prologue to the Millian era of constitutional liberties:

> [T]he task of translating the majestic generalities of the Bill of Rights, conceived as part of the pattern of liberal government in the eighteenth century, into concrete restraints on officials dealing with the problems of the twentieth century, is one to disturb self-confidence. These principles grew in soil which also produced a philosophy that the individual was the center of society, that his liberty was attainable through the mere absence of governmental restraints, and that government should be entrusted with few controls and only the mildest supervision over men's affairs. We must translate these rights to a soil in which the laissez-faire concept or principle of non-interference has withered at least as to economic affairs, and social advancements are increasingly sought through closer integration of society and expanded and strengthened governmental controls. These changed conditions often deprive precedents of reliability and cast us more than we would choose upon our own judgment... We cannot... withhold the judgment that history authenticates as the function of this Court when liberty is infringed.[80]

The new "liberty" was very different from the old, with implications for the personal or "private" sphere, for freedom of expression and for equality. The two clauses left intact by the *Slaughterhouse* cases, Due Process and Equal Protection, along with the First Amendment would become a tripartite expression of this newer idea of liberty.

[78] 301 US 1 (1937).

[79] *West Virginia State Board of Education* v. *Barnette*, 319 US 624 (1943).

[80] 319 US at 639–40.

5

The Intellectual Origins of the Right to Privacy

When the Supreme Court overruled *Lochner* and its progeny, it did not – for long, at least – discontinue using the Due Process clause and other constitutional provisions to protect un-enumerated constitutional rights. Within a few years it began to work out the contours of a new conception of personal freedom, one with very different social and political ramifications than the older, classical liberal ideal exemplified by *Lochner.* Central to the more recent idea of liberty is the notion of expressive self-individuation. When expressed in constitutional terms, this ideal has three dimensions: First, there must be an individual realm which is, as much as possible, free from governmental and social influences – a realm of privacy in which the individual can "become himself" and live the kind of life he or she wishes. Second, the individual must be free to express his ideas, opinions, thoughts and – in the deepest sense – *himself* in the non-private sphere. Third, there must prevail social conditions of basic equality so that each individual has roughly the same opportunities as everyone else to achieve their goals and to create their own style of life.

Each of the next three chapters explores these respective dimensions of Mill's thought and his influence on the modern American constitutional tradition. In this chapter, we discuss Mill's influence leading to the recognition of the constitutional right to privacy.

THE "HARM PRINCIPLE"

In Chapter I of *On Liberty,* Mill sought to develop and deploy a hermetic principle separating the realm of public authority from the domain of individual freedom. He began by dividing the world of human activity into two spheres – the "self-regarding" and the "other-regarding." Society has the right to interfere only in the latter sphere:

> The only part of the conduct of anyone for which he is amenable to society is that which concerns others. In the part which only concerns himself, his

> independence is, of right, absolute. Over himself, over his own body and mind, the individual is sovereign.[1]

Unlike the classical liberal notion of freedom, which applied only to government, Mill's harm principle applied to *society* as well. Indeed, he thought social coercion could be far more invasive than merely legal restrictions. This is where Mill's concern about the "tyranny of the majority" was strongest. He insisted that society "practices a social tyranny more formidable than many forms of political oppression since ... it leaves fewer means of escape, penetrating much more deeply into the details of life and enslaving the soul itself."[2]

In its essence, the "harm principle" provides that society and government may not legitimately interfere with individual freedom except to protect third parties from some specific harm caused by the prohibited action.[3] To "harm" another, in Mill's specific sense, is to violate the individual's moral or legal interests.[4] Merely offensive conduct, for example, does not qualify as harmful though Mill made certain concessions to the moral traditions of our society. He allowed, for example, that the state could prohibit public indecency even though it might not constitute a harm, strictly speaking.[5]

But in other ways, he held the line on what constituted a "harm." In his view, a person is not "harmed," for example, when a loved-one's self-destructive behavior causes them severe emotional distress.[6] Nor does some generalized or merely probabilistic threat of harm justify interference.[7] The fact that a red-light district might attract a criminal element, or that the legalization of marijuana (to take a contemporary example) might be expected to lead to lowered social productivity or a rise in traffic accidents is too indirect, too generalized and/or too speculative to qualify as a bona fide harm under his principle. While the state can restrict the behavior of *particular individuals* who have caused a public harm through drunk driving or drug

[1] John Stuart Mill, *On Liberty, CW*, 18:224.

[2] Ibid., 219–20.

[3] "The sole end for which mankind are warranted, individually or collectively, in interfering with the liberty of action of any of their members is self-protection." Ibid.

[4] Mill describes this as "certain interests, which either by express legal provision or tacit understanding, ought to be considered as rights." Ibid., 276. Harm was, thus, not some empirical concept equivalent to a demonstrable injury but rather, a normative concept. As such, it is open to the objection that there is a potential circularity or even vacuity here. It opens the possibility that the concept of harm could be broadened or narrowed by altering the legal protection of certain interests, or the "tacitly understood" sphere of moral interests. See J. C. Rees, "A Re-Reading of Mill *On Liberty*," in *J. S. Mill, On Liberty in Focus*, eds. John Gray and G. W. Smith (London: Routledge, 1991), 169–89 (for an extended argument concerning the potentially circular nature of Mill's idea of harm).

[5] Mill observed that "[t]here are many acts which, being directly injurious to the agents themselves, ought not to be legally interfered with but which, if done publicly, are a violation of good manners and, coming thus within the category of offenses against others, may rightly be prohibited. Of this kind are offenses against decency on which it is unnecessary to dwell...." Mill, *On Liberty, CW*, 18:295–96.

[6] Ibid., 280–81.

[7] There must be "a definite damage, or definite risk of damage, either to an individual or to the public." Ibid., 281–82. Similarly, a person cannot be interfered with for his own good "when there is not a certainty, but only a danger of mischief." Ibid., 294.

use, for example, the state cannot preemptively circumscribe the liberty of others to use these substances. Society may not, so to speak, uproot the seeds of social evils until the point at which they pose a direct and specific threat to identifiable persons.

These strictures on the meaning of "harm" entail that two traditional motives for legislation cannot be justified: legal paternalism and legal moralism. Legal paternalism, in the strict sense, is the use of law to protect an individual from the consequences of his own imprudent or self-destructive behavior. Classic examples of paternalism include motorcycle helmet and seatbelt laws, restrictions on drug use, prostitution, gambling or other putatively immoral acts to the extent that these are motivated by concern for the actors themselves. Limitations on the right to contract are often based on paternalistic justifications. Prohibitions of surrogate mother contracts or contracts to sell a vital organ such as a kidney or even a contract to work for longer hours than is thought healthful, as in the *Lochner* case, are examples. Even Social Security might be considered paternalistic to the extent that it is motivated by an effort to force the individual to set aside funds for his own retirement.[8]

Although anti-paternalism was a staple of classical liberal thought before him, Mill bolstered the case against paternalism in several ways. He insisted repeatedly that every adult is the captain of his own ship who may live his life as he sees fit irrespective of whether it is (or others think it is) healthy, prudent or conducive to his own well-being.[9] He argued that no one ought to tell another adult how to live, that the individual is likely to know his interests and plan of life far better than others, and that, when society intervenes, it usually does so ineptly.[10] He argued that to "harm" a person is to violate a duty owed to them, *but that we have no true duties to ourselves*: all rights and duties are essentially "other-regarding," *interpersonal* in nature.[11] Consequently, no person can harm himself, properly speaking. Without a duty to oneself, moreover, there is no moral or legal ground for society to interfere. The profligate who squanders his inheritance leaving nothing for old age and the drug addict who throws away his health have acted, Mill insisted, *imprudently* but not *immorally*.[12]

[8] At least it would be paternalistic if Social Security actually functioned in this way.

[9] After introducing the harm principle, Mill observed that "His own good, either physical or moral, is not a sufficient warrant. He cannot rightfully be compelled to do or forbear because it will be better for him to do so, because it will make him happier, because, in the opinion of others, to do so would be wise or even right. These are good reasons for remonstrating with him, or for reasoning with him, or persuading him, or entreating him, but not for compelling him. ..." Mill, *On Liberty*, CW, 18:223–24.

[10] Ibid., 227.

[11] Particular acts "are only a subject of moral reprobation when they involve a breach of duty *to others*. ... What are called duties to oneself are not socially obligatory unless circumstances render them at the same time duties to others. The term duty to oneself, when it means anything more than prudence, means self-respect or self-development, and for none of these is anyone accountable to his fellow creatures." Ibid., 280.

[12] Ibid., 281.

It is precisely on this point that modern liberalism departs most strikingly from Mill's ideas. Mill assumed – perhaps too optimistically – that a society that properly educated its members would not be in great need of paternalistic legislation. He charged that, if society lets a considerable share of its members "grow up mere children," it only "has itself to blame for the consequences" of the failure to properly educate them.[13] But as H. L. A. Hart, one of Mill's most enthusiastic modern defenders, nevertheless cautioned, we have become increasingly aware of the ways in which various social, biological and other heteronomous influences can effect freedom of choice.[14]

The harm principle also prohibits *moralistic* interferences with self-regarding acts.[15] Here modern liberalism is fully on board with the thrust of Mill's thought. Before Mill, many classical liberal writers followed Locke in assuming that, though government's chief end is the protection of property, nothing prevents it from helping to enforce important social and moral norms through the strategic use of law. Classical liberal constitutionalists rarely doubted that the state could prohibit adultery, prostitution, gambling, homosexuality, suicide or other acts on the basis of what was regarded as their objectionable moral character.[16] It was Bentham who began to question the efficacy of such laws on two grounds – that they were often difficult to enforce and that they undercut net utility by reducing the happiness or pleasure of those involved without conferring any utilitarian benefit. Yet Mill took a still more categorical stand. He argued specifically against laws prohibiting alcohol and opium use, fornication, prostitution and gambling on the grounds that these activities involve matters which are simply none of society's business.[17] He considered this

13 Ibid., 282.

14 Hart wrote, "I do not propose to defend all that Mill said.... No doubt if we no longer sympathize with this criticism [of paternalism in regard to drug laws] this is due, in part, to a general decline in the belief that individuals no their own interests best and to an increased awareness of a great range of factors which diminish the significance to be attached to an apparently free choice or consent.... Underlying Mill's extreme fear of paternalism there perhaps is a conception of what a normal human being is like which now seems not to correspond to the facts. Mill, in fact, endows him with too much of the psychology of a middle-aged man whose desires are relatively fixed." H. L. A. Hart, *Law, Liberty and Morality* (Stanford: Stanford University Press, 1963), 5, 32–33.

15 Moralistic legislation are laws which prohibit or regulate not because the activity is harmful but because it is thought to be immoral by the majority. See H. L. A. Hart, *Law, Liberty and Morality* (Stanford: Stanford University Press, 1963) for a classic modern liberal attack on morals legislation.

16 As Christopher Tiedeman put it, the police power of the state includes the power to say regulate the "health, safety and morals" of the community. Christopher G. Tiedeman, *A Treatise on the Limitations of the Police Power in the United States*. This issue is one of the points that divides classical liberals from modern libertarians. As a leading libertarian commentator puts it, "The right of self-ownership certainly implies the right to decide for ourselves what food, drink, or drugs we will put into our own bodies; with whom we will make love (assuming our chosen partner agrees); and what kind of medical treatment we want (assuming a doctor agrees to provide it). David Boaz, *Libertarianism* (New York; London: The Free Press, 1997), 79.

17 Mill, *On Liberty*, *CW*, 18:297–99.

particularly true in matters involving sexual relations between adults. Indeed, five years before *On Liberty* was published, he wrote in his diary that he was "anxious to have on record" his view that "what any person may freely do with respect to sexual relations should be deemed to be an unimportant and purely private matter."[18]

Mill did qualify or limit some of his conclusions. While prostitution should not be prohibited, public solicitation, pandering and pimping could be regulated, he thought, to ensure that the customer's decisions are "as free as possible from the art of persons who stimulate their inclinations."[19] (Of course, this reasoning is itself paternalistic insofar as the law seeks to shield the individual from conditions that might adversely affect his choices.) Similarly, alcohol should not be prohibited nor should the number of taverns be legally restricted by zoning laws. But alcohol may be taxed since government can legitimately prioritize among the commodities it chooses to burden by taxation.[20] Anyone, moreover, who commits a violent act while intoxicated can legitimately be prohibited from alcohol use with escalating penalties in the event of non-compliance.[21] These conclusions can almost certainly be extended to the debate about drug legalization today.[22]

On other issues, he advocated only the mildest of limits on individual activity. He argued for moderate restrictions on the sale of guns.[23] More generally, while each person can contract with others freely for any act or service that does not harm a third party, a person may not sell himself into involuntary servitude because this one act of self-disposal negates all of the other free choices that the individual might potentially have made in the future.[24] Although he was an ardent feminist, he concluded that the state may not prohibit polygamy since such relationships are voluntary among adults.[25] It is also a safe conjecture that Mill would have fully supported gay marriage today. Indeed, as we will see in Chapter 6, this conclusion flows from his (and Harriet's) insistence that all persons should be absolutely free in matters of marriage and divorce.

18 John Stuart Mill, "Diary, 1854," in *Journals and Debating Speeches Part II (1827)*, CW, 27:664 (entry of March 26, 1854).

19 Mill, *On Liberty*, CW, 18:297.

20 Ibid., 298.

21 Ibid., 295.

22 Mill went so far as to argue that laws prohibiting the importation of opium into China, which were passed in the wake of an epidemic of addiction, were an infringement on the liberty of the user. Ibid., 294–95.

23 The seller could be required to take down the name and address of the buyer, along with the reasons given for the purchase. Ibid., at 295.

24 Mill, *On Liberty*, CW, 18:299. Of course, many forms of paternalism can now be justified on this qualification. The individual can be prohibited from smoking or using drugs or a thousand other activities which Mill wanted to protect on the ground that these activities are liberty-negating in the long run. For this reason, other more thorough-going libertarians have not stopped short of permitting contracts to sell oneself into servitude.

25 Ibid., 290.

THE PERSONAL SPHERE: THREE CORE FREEDOMS

These considerations summarize the "harm principle" from society's side. They define what the government and society generally may not touch. Further, Mill also took up the question of which freedoms should be protected from the individual's side. Within the self-regarding sphere, he argued that three zones of human liberty should be absolutely free from all restrictions and sanctions, political or social.

The first of these concerns the freedom to think and believe whatever one wishes, along with the right to speak one's convictions without fear of punishment or informal sanction. Mill called this "liberty of conscience in the most comprehensive sense." This freedom embraces "absolute freedom of opinion and sentiment on all subjects, practical or speculative, scientific, moral and theological."[26] He understood this first sphere of liberty to encompass not simply the inner domain of conscience and opinion, but also an unlimited freedom of "expressing and publishing opinions" since this is "practically inseparable" from liberty of thought.[27]

The second zone to be protected involves our self-regarding *actions*. We possess, Mill argued, a "liberty of tastes and pursuits, of framing the plan of our life to suit our character."[28] This is the right to make decisions, to plan for one's life, the right not to be coerced or unduly influenced into doing things which are alien to one's own life plan. It is the right to undertake a course of life which suits one's character and which nurtures the unfolding of one's true self. Here is the core of the negative liberal ideal of freedom, the impetus for what Justice Brandeis would call in the twentieth century the "right to be let alone."[29]

The third zone of liberty was interpersonal, the "freedom to unite for any purpose not involving harm to other persons."[30] Mill was proposing a general right of association far more expansive than prevailing ideas such as the right to assemble to petition government, which is codified in our First Amendment. He was arguing for the protection of what Tocqueville called "secondary associations" of every kind – political, social, artistic, scientific, cultural and personal. The free and autonomous individual has a right to unite with other free and autonomous individuals for any non-harmful purpose.

These three zones of liberty would come to represent the heart of the right to privacy as it was developed by the Supreme Court in the twentieth century.

26 Ibid., 225.
27 Ibid.
28 Ibid., 226.
29 *Olmstead* v. *United States*, 277 US at 490 (Brandeis, J., dissenting).
30 Mill, *On Liberty*, *CW*, 18:226.

FROM THE "HARM PRINCIPLE" TO THE RIGHT TO PRIVACY

A full century stands between the publication of *On Liberty* and the birth of the constitutional right to privacy with *Griswold* v. *Connecticut* in 1965.[31] But this was not because the book was not immediately influential. To the contrary, *On Liberty* was an instant classic. Six editions appeared during the remaining fourteen years of Mill's life. Within a decade of its publication, hundreds of thousands in the United Kingdom and the United States had read it. The book was also translated into several other languages. Indeed, so famous was the book a decade or so after its publication that a young Sigmund Freud translated it into German for his own edification in the early 1870s.[32]

Before long, the book began to influence scholars and legal thinkers as they began to grope their way toward articulating a workable conception of privacy for the modern age.[33] The first important expression of this impulse in the United States was a law review article entitled "The Right to Privacy" published in the *Harvard Law Review* in 1890 by Charles Warren and the future Justice Brandeis.[34] This article argued for the creation not of a constitutional right against the government, but of a *tort* right of privacy providing remedies against third parties for the unwanted publication of private correspondence, information and photographs, etc.

Brandeis is one of at least four United States Supreme Court justices – the others were Oliver Wendell Holmes, Jr., William O. Douglas and, more recently, Anthony Kennedy – who were deeply familiar with Mill and were, indeed, directly influenced by him. The Warren and Brandeis' article clearly bears the hallmarks of Mill's notion of privacy. Born in 1856, a biographer describes Brandeis' childhood and family as one "enamored with books, music and politics."[35] *On Liberty* appeared when he was three years old and it is almost certain that Brandeis read the book as a young man. He graduated Harvard law school at the age of twenty, in the mid-1870s, at a point when Mill's influence was near its apogee in the United States. Later in life, Brandeis mentioned Mill in two letters written during the

[31] 381 US 479 (1965). There had been other developments on the privacy front during the intervening century. Tort lawyers began to develop a "right to privacy" protecting private spaces and private information. The catalyst for this was the most frequently cited law review article of all time. Samuel D. Warren and Louis D. Brandeis, "The Right to Privacy," 4 *Harv. L. Rev.* 5 (1890). By mid-twentieth century, courts had begun to recognize these rights. See William L. Prosser, "Privacy," 48 *Calif. L. Rev.* 383 (1960). As a sitting Supreme Court justice, Brandeis argued in dissent for a constitutional "right to be let alone" analogous to the privacy right. *Olmstead* v. *United States*, 277 US 438 (1928). And five years before Griswold, Justice Harlan had written a famous dissent in *Poe* v. *Ullman*, 367 US 497 (1961) (arguing that the due process clause protects private acts against the same Connecticut statute as was at issue in Griswold).

[32] Erich Fromm, *Sigmund Freud's Mission: An Analysis of His Personality and Influence* (London: G. Allen and Unwin, 1959), 96.

[33] The very term "privacy" connotes several different ideas…

[34] Charles Warren and Louis D. Brandeis, "The Right to Privacy," 4 *Harvard Law Review* 193 (1890).

[35] John R. Vile, *Great American Judges: An Encyclopedia* (Santa Barbara: ABC-CLIO, 2003).

spring of 1928, paraphrasing closely in one written to his personal secretary from Mill's *Considerations on Representative Government*: "Tell your doubting friends: one man with a conviction is more powerful than 99 who have only interests."[36]

The authors of "The Right to Privacy" railed against the trivializing influences of gossip and the stuff of cheap tabloids.[37] The verbiage of the article seems to channel Mill's high-toned contempt for all things small and idle, and his aristocratic embrace of all things that nurture the nobler human emotions. They wrote: "Triviality destroys at once robustness of thought and delicacy of feeling. No enthusiasm can flourish, no generous impulse can survive under its blighting influence."[38] Mill's warnings against the way in which social and interpersonal influences can subtly, but coercively, invade the recesses of the soul – are reflected in the creation of a tort right that would protect the individual against non-political actors.

Even more persuasively, however, Warren and Brandeis cast this new right not on the foundations of a quasi-property right analogous to common law protection against theft or copyright infringements, but on the basis of a *personal right of self-determination* – a right of "inviolate personality."[39] The authors located the source of this right in "a more general right to be let alone."[40] They borrowed this phrase from the most celebrated constitutional theorist of the late nineteenth century, Thomas Cooley,[41] a Michigan jurist who had written perhaps the most influential constitutional treatise of the post–Civil War period.[42]

36 Brandeis to Alice Harriet Grady (May 13, 1928) in Louis Brandeis, et al., *Letters of Louis D. Brandeis Vol. 5: 1921–1941 – Elder Statesman*, ed. Melvin I. Urofsky and David W. Levy (Albany: SUNY Press, 1978), 340, https://perma.cc/4ZU9-NLCE. Brandeis to Jacob H. Gilbert (April 18, 1928) in *The Family Letters of Louis D. Brandeis*, ed. Melvin I. Urofsky and David W. Levy (Norman: University of Oklahoma Press, 2002), 464.

37 Warren and Brandeis, "The Right to Privacy," 196.

38 Ibid.

39 "The principle which protects personal writings and all other personal production, not against theft and personal appropriation, but against publication in any form, is in reality not the principle of private property but that of an inviolate personality." Ibid., 205. "The common law secures to each person *the right of determining, ordinarily, to what extent his thoughts, sentiments and emotions shall be communicated to others*." Ibid., 198 (emphasis added).

40 Ibid., 193.

41 Ibid.

42 Cooley's *Constitutional Limitations* was published in 1868, almost a decade after *On Liberty* had been published and the year the Fourteenth Amendment was ratified. Cooley was a defender of strict limits on federal power and the idea that would become popular during the Lochner era, that the due process clause protects basic economic rights – freedom of contract and property. Thomas M. Cooley, *Constitutional Limitations*, 8th ed. (Boston: Little, Brown, and Co., 1927). We do not know whether Cooley had read Mill. His ideas owed more to the classical liberal influence. For example, he defended the right of the state to legislate to protect health, safety *and morals*. Ibid., 1223–338. But his notion of a "right to be let alone" is one of those conceptual bridges from the older to the newer liberalism. See J. L. Hill, "The Five Faces of Freedom in American Political and Constitutional Thought," 45 *Boston College L. Rev.* 499, 532–33 (2004) (discussing Cooley's influence in the shift from the classical liberal to modern notions of freedom).

Warren and Brandeis' article (which has been called the most oft-cited law review article of all time) spurred the development of a new tort right of privacy which gradually gained recognition over the course of the twentieth century.[43] The new tort right of privacy, as it was developed and elaborated by courts in different situations, included four distinct tort privacy causes of action: the publication of private facts and photos, the invasion of private spaces, "false light" publication which distorts true information and creates a false perception of the victim, and misappropriation of name and likeness.[44] Even though these were tort rights, not constitutional rights, their acceptance by American courts in the twentieth century signaled a growing recognition of the need to protect privacy in all of its various facets.[45] They also provided a remedy for infringement by private actors, those who are not covered by the Constitution in any event.

Warren and Brandeis' reference to the "right to be let alone" was significant, however, not only because it elucidated the deeper and more general nature of the source of the privacy right they were proposing, but also because, almost forty years later, Brandeis would – now as a Justice on the US Supreme Court – resurrect this phrase in one of his most famous constitutional dissents. In *Olmstead* v. *United States*,[46] a case involving the conviction of bootleggers using evidence obtained by warrantless telephone wiretapping, Brandeis argued in dissent that there is "a right to be let alone" which should inform our understanding of the Fourth Amendment right against searches and seizures.[47] Telephone conversations were private and should be off-limits to government without a warrant. Significantly, the decision in *Olmstead* was announced in early June 1928. Brandeis would have been writing his dissent during the preceding month or two which was precisely the period when he had written the two previously mentioned letters referencing Mill, in April and May 1928, respectively. It seems likely that he was re-reading Mill, perhaps looking

43 New York State passed the first statute protecting a tort right of privacy in 1903. Victor E. Schwartz, Kathryn Kelly and David F. Partlett, *Torts: Cases and Materials* (New York: Foundation Press), supra note – at 976. Many courts came to accept the tort both as a protection for private places, *Pearson* v. *Dodd*, 420 F. 2d 701, D.C. Cir. (1969), and publication of private photos and information, *Flake* v. *Greensboro News Co.*, 195 S.E. 55 (1938). "At the present time, the right to privacy is clearly recognized ... in one form or another, in all but two or three states." Schwartz, Kelly and Partlett, *Torts*, at 977.

44 Just five years before the elaboration of the constitutional right, Prosser wrote an important article delineating the four varieties of the tort right of privacy. See William L. Prosser, "Privacy," 48 *California Law Review* 383 (1960) (distinguishing invasion of private places, publication of private information, the "false light" privacy tort, where true information is placed in a false light damaging to plaintiff's reputation, and misappropriation of name or likeness, where plaintiff's name or likeness is used for commercial purposes).

45 Warren and Brandeis, "The Right to Privacy."

46 277 US 478 (1928).

47 Ibid., 490 (Brandeis, J., dissenting). This decision, decided on a 5–4 basis, was later overruled in *Katz* v. *United States*, 389 US 347 (1967). Justice Brandeis's principle – and, more indirectly, Mill's – was thus later vindicated.

for inspiration for his "right to be let alone," during that period of time. At any rate, Brandeis' "right to be let alone" – even if invoked in dissent – was the first genuine *constitutional* invocation of a right to privacy.

THE ROAD TO GRISWOLD

Brandeis' *Olmstead* dissent came in 1928, toward the end of the Lochner era. By 1937, as we saw in the last chapter, the Court had given up using the Due Process clause to protect freedom of contract even as it conceded a much broader role for federal power in the economic sphere under the commerce clause. Together, these two developments signaled the decline of special protections for economic liberties. But even as the Court ceased protecting economic liberties, it began to single out other rights for special protection – rights connected to personal autonomy.

In 1942, the Court decided its first important post-*Lochner* individual rights case, *Skinner* v. *Oklahoma*.[48] In the first decades of the twentieth century, eugenics statutes had been passed in most of the states. Some of these statutes, like Oklahoma's, operated on the theory that criminality was a genetically transmissible trait. The statute at issue in *Skinner* provided that anyone convicted at least three times for crimes involving "moral turpitude" could be involuntarily sterilized. Skinner had been thrice convicted for petty theft and other lesser criminal offenses and was sentenced to forced sterilization.

Justice William O. Douglas wrote the decision in *Skinner*. Appointed as a New Deal supporter by F.D.R., Douglas, too, had read and internalized his Mill. He quoted him frequently, most often in the context of freedom of expression.[49] But Douglas's biographer has noted that Douglas's idea of a right of privacy was "also derived from the classical liberalism associated with John Stuart Mill."[50] Indeed, we will see just how much shortly.

The *Skinner* decision recognized a right to procreate under the Equal Protection clause of the Fourteenth Amendment. Of course, a "right to procreate" is mentioned nowhere in the Constitution, and the Equal Protection clause

48 316 US 535 (1942).

49 In *Anatomy of Liberty: The Rights of Man without Force*, Douglas makes note of both Mill's and Jefferson's opinions on freedom of expression:

> "Jefferson's theory and the idea espoused by the Britisher, John Stuart Mill, have common ground. Mill wrote, 'If all mankind minus one, were of one opinion, and only one person were of the contrary opinion, mankind would be no more justified in silencing that one person, than he, if he had the power, would be justified in silencing mankind.' This does not mean of course that a person can slander or libel another. Exceptions for slander and libel as well as obscenity have deep roots in American law."

William O. Douglas, *The Rights of Man without Force* (New York: Simon and Schuster, 1963), 8. We will discuss Mill's influence on Douglas in the context of freedom of expression in the next chapter.

50 Stephen L. Wasby, *"He Shall Not Pass This Way Again": The Legacy of Justice William O. Douglas* (Pittsburgh: University of Pittsburgh Press, 1990), 167.

might seem a strange place to locate this new right. But the more likely basis for the right, the Due Process clause, was recently out of favor with the Court due to its association with *Lochner*. Douglas ingeniously sensed that the value of equality would assume a new significance in the modern constitutional order. His choice of the Equal Protection clause thus resonated with the emerging philosophy while avoiding the taint of *Lochner*. He wrote in the majority opinion:

> Marriage and procreation are fundamental to the very existence and survival of the race. The power to sterilize, if exercised, may have subtle, far-reaching and devastating effects. In evil or reckless hands, it can cause races or types which are inimical to the dominant group to wither and disappear. There is no redemption for the individual whom the law touches.[51]

The impact on the right to procreate, he continued, fell unequally on different groups. The petty thief or the "blue collar" criminal could be sterilized for stealing twenty dollars, while politicians guilty of graft or extortion were exempt from the statute.

Skinner was the first of several "fundamental interest" cases in which the Equal Protection clause was used in place of Due Process – just so long as some inequality could be found. The real "work" – the substance of the right – was the newly discovered "right to procreate." But, crucially, even this right could be linked to the older, more traditional kinds of rights protected in cases such as *Meyer* v. *Nebraska* and *Pierce* v. *Society of Sisters*, the two Lochner era cases that touch upon the right of family autonomy. Each of these cases – *Meyer*, *Pierce* and *Skinner* – would in turn be built upon to develop the privacy right that would follow twenty years later.

In 1961, the Supreme Court had its first opportunity to unveil the privacy right. It was a failed attempt, but still significant for what it would say about privacy. Connecticut had passed a law in 1879 prohibiting the sale, distribution or use of contraceptive devices. The law was a state offshoot of the federal Comstock Act of 1873, which prohibited the distribution in the US mails of "obscene" material – which included publications concerning methods of birth control. The plaintiffs in this case, *Poe* v. *Ulman*,[52] sought a declaratory judgment from the Court that the law was unconstitutional. The majority dismissed the appeal challenging the laws, holding that the case was nonjusticiable – a term constitutional lawyers use to denote cases where there exists no real present controversy to be decided by a court. There had been only one prosecution under the law in the eighty years of its existence, and this had resulted in a dismissal twenty years earlier, in 1940. The Court essentially declined to rule because they believed there was no real threat of prosecution under the law.

Missed opportunity though it was, several justices dissented from the dismissal, leaving powerful arguments that would be resuscitated a few years later. Justice

[51] 316 US at 541.
[52] 367 US 497 (1961)

Harlan penned a now-famous dissent, arguing for the first time that the Due Process clause protects a zone of liberty broader than those liberties picked out by specific provisions of the Constitution:

> The full scope of the liberty guaranteed by the Due Process Clause cannot be found in or Limited by the precise terms of the specific guarantees elsewhere provided in the Constitution. This liberty *is not a series of isolated points picked out in terms of the taking of property, the freedom of speech, press and religion, the right to keep and bear arms in the United States, the freedom from unreasonable searches and seizures,* and so on. It is a rational continuum which, broadly speaking, includes a freedom from all substantial arbitrary impositions and purposeless restraints.[53]

Harlan was suggesting that there is *one central, underlying concept of freedom* protected by the Due Process Clause, not several distinct and discrete constitutional rights. If this is so, then there must be one principle that defines this freedom – a principle he did not name but which embraces freedom from all "arbitrary impositions" and "purposeless restraints" – a principle that portends a broadly Millian understanding of freedom.

Justice Douglas, who had authored the *Skinner* opinion, wrote a stirring dissent in which he quoted Mill directly:

> Leveling the discourse of medical men to the morality of a particular community is a deadening influence. Mill spoke of the pressures of intolerant groups that produce 'either mere conformers to commonplace, or time servers for truth. … The chronicles are filled with sad attempts of government to stomp out ideas, to ban thoughts because they are heretical or obnoxious. As Mill stated, "Our merely social intolerance kills no one, rots out no opinions, but induces men to disguise them, or to abstain from any active effort for their diffusion." When that happens society suffers.[54]

The broader passage expresses many of Mill's central themes – the need for social experimentation, the stultifying influence of rigid moralism, the link between prohibition of certain activities and the corseting of thought and discussion where that activity is concerned. Douglas even quoted a theologian who, though he thought use of contraception a sin, believed that the use of contraceptives was a matter of morality, not legality – and, thus, none of the law's business.[55]

Four years later, in *Griswold* v. *Connecticut*, the Court revisited – and, this time, struck down – that same Connecticut law.[56] During the interim, two justices in the *Poe* majority were replaced by more liberal judges. Justice Frankfurter, who had written the majority opinion in *Poe* dismissing the case, had died and was replaced

[53] Ibid., at 546 (Harlan, J., dissenting) (my emphasis).
[54] 367 US at 514 (Douglas, J., dissenting) (quoting *On Liberty*).
[55] Ibid., at 515.
[56] 381 US 479 (1965).

by Justice Goldberg, who voted to recognize a right to privacy. And Justice Whitaker was replaced by Justice White, who voted with the majority in *Griswold*, though on narrower grounds.

Again, it was Justice Douglas who wrote the first and still most frequently discussed of the various opinions in *Griswold.* He argued that the right to privacy is found in the "penumbras and emanations" of various other constitutional rights: the First Amendment right of association, the Third Amendment right against quartering soldiers in houses, the Fourth Amendment right against searches and seizures (quoting, with approval, Brandeis' "right to be let alone" dissent in *Olmstead*), the Fifth Amendment right against self-incrimination and the implications of the Ninth and Fourteenth Amendment's due process clause.[57] The "penumbras and emanations" idea was Douglas' novel attempt to find a deeper philosophical principle uniting, but also transcending, the various provisions of the Bill of Rights. As commentators have pointed out, the various amendments he cited protect "privacy" in different senses. The Third and Fourth Amendments protect private *places* – the home – whereas the Fifth Amendment's self-incrimination clause protects privacy of conscience even as the First Amendment's protection of the right of association protects interpersonal privacy, that is, the privacy of individuals to unite for political, social or even personal reasons.

Though often criticized,[58] Justice Douglas's approach resolves two distinct though interrelated issues – one constitutional, the other philosophical – facing the creation of a new right to privacy. The constitutional issue concerns where the privacy right derives from in the Constitution whereas the philosophical issue concerns which activities, exactly, are protected by the right. Since the Constitution makes no mention of a privacy right, the right cannot be located in one or another textual provision of the Constitution. Douglas's answer is that *there is no one provision protecting privacy because the privacy principle is a more fundamental idea of liberty* that animates (and unites) the more specific provisions of the Bill of Rights. His argument is that, while the particular provisions of the Bill of Rights are specifically circumscribed to ensure that the spheres of activity most likely, in the Framers' experience, to be infringed by government – the right of privacy in the home, the right to liberty of conscience, freedom of association and the rest – they are not the whole or the essence of liberty.

57 381 US at 481–82.

58 Indeed, some criticized the idea of privacy as fundamentally vague. As Louis Henkin wrote:

> Justice Douglas's argument seems to go something like this: since the Constitution in various "specifics" of the Bill of Rights and in their penumbra, protect rights which partake of privacy, it protects … a general, complete right to privacy. But the opposite might be true, that when the Constitution sought to protect private rights, it specified them; that it explicitly protects some elements of privacy, but not others, suggests that it did not mean to protect those not mentioned."

Louis Henkin, "Privacy and Autonomy," 74 *Columbia Law Review* 1410, 142–22 (1974) (arguing that the real value protected by Griswold and *Roe* v. *Wade* was autonomy); see Comment, "A Taxonomy of Privacy: Repose, Sanctuary and Intimate Decision," 64 *Calif. L. Rev.*, 1447, 1448 (1976) (arguing that privacy is actually a constellation of these three distinct values).

Other justices took a more conservative tack, locating the right in various other textual provisions of the Constitution – the Ninth or Fourteenth Amendment.[59] Most steered clear of explicitly connecting the right to privacy with a quasi-Millian right. Several opinions linked the right in this case to a more limited right of family autonomy, the kind of right protected in *Meyer* v. *Nebraska* and *Pierce* v. *Society of Sisters*. Even Justice Douglas insisted that the new right was connected to the conjugal rights of a married couple:

> We deal with a right to privacy *older than the Bill of Rights*. [Marriage] is a coming together for better or for worse, hopefully enduring, and intimate to the degree of being sacred. It is an association that promotes a way of life, not causes; a harmony in living, not political faiths; a bilateral loyalty, not commercial or social projects.[60]

And Justice Harlan, whose dissent in *Poe* v. *Ullman* presaged *Griswold*, went out of his way to distance his conception of privacy from the anti-moralistic consequences of the harm principle, observing, "I would not suggest that adultery, homosexuality, fornication and incest are immune from criminal enquiry."[61]

Griswold, in sum, was a foot in the door.

The limited conception of privacy which *Griswold* envisioned was, indeed, short-lived. In *Eisenstadt* v. *Baird*,[62] a case decided in 1972, seven years after *Griswold*, the Court held unconstitutional a Massachusetts law which prohibited the distribution of contraception to *unmarried* persons. Baird had given a lecture on birth control methods and had given away contraceptives to audience members at the end of his discussion.

A plurality of the Court, in an opinion written by Justice Brennan, joined by Douglas, Stewart and Marshall, used the Equal Protection clause, rather than the Due Process clause, holding that there was no rational reason for treating married and unmarried persons differently. In sum, the *Griswold* right could not be reserved for married persons only. But the heart of the opinion sounds in Due Process for the Court asserted that the right to use contraceptives is an *individual* right based on the individual's fundamental interest in autonomy:

> It is true that in *Griswold* the right of privacy in question inhered in the *marital* relationship. Yet the marital couple is not an independent entity with a mind and heart of its own, but an association of two individuals each with a separate intellectual and emotional makeup. If the right of privacy means anything, it is the right

59 Whereas Justice Douglas argued that the right arose from the "penumbras and emanations" of the First, Third, Fourth, Fifth and Fourteenth Amendments, 381 US at 481; Justice Goldberg thought that the Ninth and Fourteenth Amendments were the basis, Ibid., at 491–94; Justice Harlan insisted that the due process clause of the Fourteenth Amendment "standing on its own bottom." Ibid., at 500.

60 381 US at 486 (my italics). The right was ancient, it was still a *marital* right – a right that depended on the association of two spouses – rather than an individual right.

61 381 US at 501.

62 405 US 438 (1972).

> *of the individual*, married or single, to be free from unwarranted governmental intrusion into matters so fundamentally affecting a person as the decision whether to bear or beget a child.[63]

Justice Brennan also waived off the putative purpose of the law – "to protect purity, to preserve chastity, to encourage continence and self-restraint" – as patently moralistic.[64] He wrote that it "would be plainly unreasonable to assume that Massachusetts has prescribed pregnancy and the birth of an unwanted child as punishment for fornication."[65]

Justice Douglas also wrote a separate concurrence arguing that Baird's acts were protected on First Amendment freedom of speech grounds. There could be no doubt that the lecture itself is protected by the First Amendment, Douglas pointed out, and giving away an item about which the lecture was concerned was part of this protection. Yet even this broad freedom of expression protection was connected, in Douglas's view, to the value of personal autonomy:

> Our system of government requires that we have faith in the ability of the individual to decide wisely, if only he is fully apprised of the merits of a controversy. … Freedom of discussion, if it would fulfill its historic function in this nation, must embrace all issues about which information is needed or appropriate to enable the members of society to cope with the exigencies of their period.[66]

Mill had said precisely the same thing a century earlier.[67]

Five years later, in *Carey* v. *Population Services*,[68] the Court extended the developing logic of the privacy right, striking down a New York law that prohibited the sale of contraceptives to persons under the age of sixteen.[69] The privacy right was defined in terms of a "field" of activity that concerns "the most intimate of human activities and relationships, decisions whether to accomplish or to prevent conception are among the most private and sensitive."[70] Reaffirming the *individual* nature of the right, Justice Brennan wrote:

> *Griswold* may no longer be read as holding only that a State may not prohibit a married couple's use of contraceptives. Read in light of its progeny, the teaching of Griswold is that the Constitution protects individual decisions in matters of childbearing from unjustified intrusion by the State.[71]

63 Eisenstadt, 405 US at 453.
64 Eisenstadt, quoting *Commonwealth* v. *Allison*, 227 Mass. 57.
65 Eisenstadt, 405 US at 448.
66 Ibid., at 457.
67 "If people must be allowed, in what only concerns themselves, to act as seems best to themselves at their own peril, they must equally be free to consult with one another about what is fit to be so done, to exchange opinions, and give and receive suggestions. Whatever it is permitted to do, it must be permitted to advise to do." Mill, *On Liberty*, CW, 18:296.
68 431 US 678 (2010).
69 *Carey* v. *Population Services*, 431 US 678 (1977).
70 Ibid., at 685.
71 Ibid., at 687.

These cases mark the true departure from the older idea, consistent with the classical liberal tradition, that government power is limited by the independence of the *family unit*, to the newer idea of privacy as an *individual* right of autonomy analogous to the harm principle.

Of course, the most far-reaching and (still) controversial of all the privacy right cases was *Roe* v. *Wade*, decided a year after *Eisenstadt*, in 1973. *Roe* established a constitutional right to abortion. Justice Blackman argued that, from the standpoint of the woman, abortion appears to fall squarely into the skein of rights related to marriage and procreation protected by earlier cases.

> This right of privacy, whether it be founded in the Fourteenth Amendment's concept of personal liberty and restrictions upon state action, as we feel it is, or, as the District Court determined, in the Ninth Amendment's reservation of rights to the people, is broad enough to encompass a woman's decision whether or not to terminate her pregnancy. The detriment that the State would impose upon the pregnant woman by denying this choice altogether is apparent. Specific and direct harm medically diagnosable even in early pregnancy may be involved. Maternity, or additional offspring, may force upon the woman a distressful life and future. Psychological harm may be imminent. Mental and physical health may be taxed by child care. There is also the distress, for all concerned, associated with the unwanted child, and there is the problem of bringing a child into a family already unable, psychologically and otherwise, to care for it. In other cases, as in this one, the additional difficulties and continuing stigma of unwed motherhood may be involved.[72]

The burden of having to raise additional offspring, the psychological difficulties attendant to child care, the stigma of unwed motherhood, along with the more palpable medical effects of pregnancy are all aspects of the privacy right. Thus, the right partakes of both a negative right to be free of physical restraint and a positive right to autonomy inherent in the idea that one should be able to construct and follow one's own life plan.

Yet from the standpoint of the fetus, the practice of abortion presents a conundrum: The harm principle, of course, prohibits harm to third parties. A person has a right to act autonomously up to the point where their act causes such harm. But is the fetus a "third party" who can be "harmed"? Put differently, is the act of abortion really "private" in a morally or constitutionally relevant sense?

Though couched in various exceptions, the Court's answer is unambiguous. It held that the fetus is not a "person" within the meaning of the Due Process clause of the Fourteenth Amendment.[73] Yet Roe's trimester framework does assume that the *state* has an interest in the "potential life" of the fetus. Before viability, the woman's right outweighs the state's interest in the unborn. Between viability (which usually occurs around twenty-four to twenty-eight weeks of pregnancy) and birth, the state's interest in protecting the unborn becomes compelling, theoretically outweighing

[72] *Roe* v. *Wade*, 410 US 113, 153 (1973).
[73] 410 US at 158.

her right. Yet even during this period, if the woman's "life or health" is in danger, the state may not prohibit abortion. In sum, only at birth does a human being become a "person" in the full constitutional sense. And up to the point of birth, the state may not prohibit abortion so long as there is a threat to the life or health of the woman.[74]

It was in a companion case to *Roe* decided on the same day, however,[75] that Justice Douglas virtually "channels" John Stuart Mill in his concurring opinion.[76] In a passage that so closely parallels Mill's discussion of the three zones of protected freedom in chapter 1 of *On Liberty* that it virtually plagiarizes him, Douglas observes that, in his view, there are three zones of liberty protected by the Fourteenth Amendment's protection of "liberty." They are "the autonomous control over the development and expression of one's intellect, interests, tastes and personality."[77] Douglas added, as Mill had, that this should be *absolutely protected*.[78] Second, there is "freedom of choice in the basic decisions of one's life respecting marriage, divorce, procreation, contraception and the education and upbringing of children."[79] While these rights are not absolute, they are subject to the rigorous protection of strict scrutiny.[80] Third, there is "the freedom to care for one's health and person, freedom from bodily restraint or compulsion, freedom to walk, stroll, or loaf."[81]

Mill's influence on Justice Douglas's thought can scarcely be doubted, as a biographer of Justice Douglas observed.[82] Douglas employed a similar special conception

74 "The fetus, at most, represents only the potentiality of life. Similarly, unborn children have been recognized as acquiring rights or interests by way of inheritance or other devolution of property, and have been represented by guardians *ad litem*. Perfection of the interests involved, again, has generally been contingent upon live birth." 410 US at 162.

75 *Doe* v. *Bolton*, 410 US 179, 209 (1973) (Douglas, J., concurring).

76 *Doe* v. *Bolton*, 410 US 179, 209 (1973) (Douglas, J., concurring).

77 Ibid., at 211. Compare Mill, whose first zone embraced "absolute freedom of opinion and sentiment on all subjects, practical or speculative, scientific, moral and theological." Mill, *On Liberty*, *CW*, 18:225.

78 Ibid.

79 Ibid. Mill's second zone embraced "the liberty of tastes and pursuits, of framing the plan of our life to suit our character." Mill, *On Liberty*, *CW*, 18:225.

80 Ibid., at 212.

81 Ibid., at 213. Only this third zone of freedom diverges from Mill's "freedom to unite for any purpose not involving harm to other persons." Since Doe involved abortion, Justice Douglas seemed to adapt Mill to the present context.

82 As Stephen Wasby observed,

> Douglas's views about the individual as the starting point for the right of privacy also derived from the classical liberalism associated with John Stuart Mill. Mill described 'A sphere of action in which society, as distinguished from the individual, has, if any, only an indirect interest; comprehending all that portion of a person's life and conduct which affects only himself.' Even the three categories of privacy which Douglas presents in his concurrence to the abortion cases derive from what Mill had described as 'the appropriate region of human liberty… First, the inward domain of consciousness;… liberty of expressing and publishing opinions… Secondly, the principle requires liberty of tastes and pursuits; of framing the plan of our life to suit our own character… Thirdly,… freedom to unite… The only freedom which deserves the name is that of pursuing our own good in our own way.'"

Wasby, *He Shall Not Pass This Way Again*, at 167.

of autonomy, insisting that "there is, of course, a sphere within which the individual may assert the supremacy of his own will and rightfully dispute the authority of any human government, especially of any free government existing under a written constitution, *to interfere with the exercise of that will.*"[83] This is deeply reminiscent of Mill's claim that "in that part which merely concerns himself, [the individual's] independence is, of right, absolute. Over himself, over his own body and mind, the individual is sovereign."[84]

During this same period of the 1970s, the Supreme Court sporadically filled out the contours of the privacy right in other contexts, using either the Due Process (directly protecting particular activities) or the Equal Protection clause (where the Court decided that a right possessed by one group could not be denied to individuals in another group, as in *Skinner* and *Eisenstadt*). In *Moore* v. *East Cleveland*, it struck down a residential zoning ordinance that limited occupancy of a dwelling to "family members," but defined "family members" in so limited a way that a grandmother was prohibited from living with two grandsons who were first cousins of each other.[85] The Court distinguished a previous case, *Belle Terra* v. *Boraas*[86] which upheld an ordinance prohibiting *non-related* persons from living together. But this case involved the right of family members to live together. Drawing from a line of cases stretching back to *Meyer* v. *Nebraska*, the Court declared:

> Our decisions establish that the Constitution protects the sanctity of the family precisely because the institution of the family is deeply rooted in this Nation's history and tradition. It is through the family that we inculcate and pass down many of our most cherished values, moral and cultural. Ours is by no means a tradition limited to respect for the bonds uniting the members of the nuclear family. The tradition of uncles, aunts, cousins, and especially grandparents sharing a household along with parents and children has roots equally venerable and equally deserving of constitutional recognition. Over the years, millions of our citizens have grown up in just such an environment, and most, surely, have profited from it. Even if conditions of modern society have brought about a decline in extended family households, they have not erased the accumulated wisdom of civilization, gained over the centuries and honored throughout our history that supports a larger conception of the family.[87]

83 410 US at 214 (emphasis added). Douglas's three zones do not parallel Mill's perfectly. Mill's third zone of liberty embraces associational rights whereas Douglas reserves his third zone for health-related decisions relevant to the kinds of cases the Court was then deciding – cases involving abortion, in particular. The first two categories of each, however, are strikingly similar, leading one to wonder if Douglas had been consciously or unconsciously influenced by Mill's discussion.

84 Mill, *On Liberty*, *CW*, 18:224.

85 431 US 494 (1977).

86 416 US 1 (1974)

87 431 US at 503–4.

A year later, the Court decided another case related to the right to marry and raise a family. In *Zablocki* v. *Redhail*, the Court struck down a Wisconsin law that required that any non-custodial parent required to pay child support had to obtain a court order showing that he or she was current in these payments before he could receive a marriage license.[88] Invoking similar privacy themes as those discussed already, the Court used a combination of the Due Process clause, protecting the right to marry, and the Equal Protection clause, which prohibits the state from drawing arbitrary lines among different classes of persons with respect to the right to marry:

> It is not surprising that the decision to marry has been placed on the same level of importance as decisions relating to procreation, childbirth, childrearing, and family relationships. As the facts of this case illustrate, it would make little sense to recognize a right of privacy with respect to other matters of family life and not with respect to the decision to enter the relationship that is the foundation of the family in our society. The woman whom appellee desired to marry had a fundamental right to seek an abortion of their expected child, *see Roe v. Wade, supra,* or to bring the child into life to suffer the myriad social, if not economic, disabilities that the status of illegitimacy brings, [cases omitted] Surely, a decision to marry and raise the child in a traditional family setting must receive equivalent protection. And, if appellee's right to procreate means anything at all, it must imply some right to enter the only relationship in which the State of Wisconsin allows sexual relations legally to take place.[89]

Ironically, this is one area in which Mill drew far more conservative conclusions than that of the Supreme Court. He concluded in *On Liberty* that "[t]he laws which, in many countries on the Continent, forbid marriage unless the parties can show that they have the means of supporting a family, do not exceed the legitimate powers of the State." And where a person fails to support existing offspring, "it is no tyranny" to force him to support his children by compulsory labor.[90]

These cases, decided in the 1960s and 1970s, represent the high-water mark of constitutional protection for the right to privacy. Though the Court continued to extend privacy protection to other activities after this point, it did so more sporadically and frequently used a lower standard of scrutiny.[91] Significantly, by the 1980s and 1990s, the courts stopped short of rigorously applying the harm principle in what would have been more recent, and perhaps more controversial, applications.

88 434 US 374 (1978).

89 43 US at 386. Zablocki relied upon *Loving* v. *Virginia*, the 1967 case which held unconstitutional laws prohibiting interracial marriage. *Loving* v. *Virginia*, 388 US 1 (1967). The *Loving* case was decided on the basis of race and Equal Protection but also, for the first time, recognized a right to marry under the Due Process clause.

90 Mill, *On Liberty*, 295.

91 It also began to use less strenuous legal standards to insulate these rights. Where "strict scrutiny was used in *Roe* v. *Wade*, for example, the Court began to employ lesser levels of protection in subsequent cases in the 1980s and beyond.

Thus, even as the courts protected contraception, abortion and other activities relating to marriage and reproduction, they consistently refused to extend privacy protection to activities such as prostitution, or possession or use of illegal drugs.[92] Perhaps more surprising, in the 1986 case of *Bowers* v. *Hardwick*, the Supreme Court, by a 5–4 vote, refused to recognize a constitutional right to engage in non-traditional sex acts such as sodomy.[93] As we will see, however, Bowers was itself overruled in 2003 in *Lawrence* v. *Texas*.

Similarly, if any activity would appear to fall squarely within an autonomy right, it would seem to be activities involving the "right to die" – either the "passive" right to refuse life-saving treatment or the "active" right to end one's life by physician-assisted suicide. Yet the Court gave little ground on this front. In the 1990 *Cruzan* case,[94] it "assumed" that there exists a "liberty interest" in the right to refuse unwanted life-sustaining medical treatment, but the decision was a pyric victory for advocates of a "right to die." Not only did the Court use a less rigorous level of scrutiny to protect what it was now calling a "liberty *interest*" (rather than a privacy *right*),[95] it upheld the highly restrictive state law which made it difficult for unconscious patients who had not left a living will or advance directive to be removed from life support.[96]

Moreover, in the 1997 case, *Washington* v. *Glucksburg*,[97] the Supreme Court held by a 9–0 vote (with some qualifications among the concurrences) that there exists no constitutional right to assisted suicide.[98] The majority specifically rejected an autonomy right, distinguishing assisted suicide from the decision to remove from oneself from ongoing medical treatment:

> The right assumed in *Cruzan*, however, was not simply deduced from abstract concepts of personal autonomy. Given the common-law rule that forced medication was a battery, and the long legal tradition protecting the decision to refuse unwanted medical treatment, our assumption was entirely consistent with this Nation's history and constitutional traditions. The decision to commit suicide with the assistance of another may be just as personal and profound as the decision to refuse unwanted medical treatment, but it has never enjoyed similar legal protection. Indeed, the two acts are widely and reasonably regarded as quite distinct.[99]

92 *B.K., Inc.* v. *Caron*, 600 F.2d 710 (1979). *Roe* v. *Butterworth*, 958 F. Supp. 1569 (1997). *Morgan* v. *City of Detroit*, 389 F. Supp. 922 (1975). Of course, Mill himself had argued that while the state may not outlaw prostitution, it could regulate the practice in various ways, that is, restricting it to appropriate zones, regulating advertising and prohibiting pimping.

93 *Bowers* v. *Hardwick*, 478 US 186 (1986).

94 *Cruzan* v. *Director*, Missouri Dept. of Health, 497 US 261 (1990).

95 Ibid., at 278.

96 The law required that, before an unconscious patient could be removed from life support, there had to be "clear and convincing evidence" that they would have wanted to be removed from life support. This standard normally cannot be met in the absence of an advance directive, such as a living will or durable power of attorney for health care.

97 521 US 702 (1997).

98 521 US at 724.

99 Ibid., at 725.

In sum, the Court rejected autonomy in favor of a more limited negative right to be free of physical constraints in the medical context – a right that had its basis in the classical liberal tradition. This was a big step back from the perspective of the autonomy right reminiscent of Mill's harm principle.

Yet the logic of the privacy-autonomy right has endured these setbacks and even *Bowers* was overruled seventeen years later in *Lawrence* v. *Texas*.[100] *Lawrence* is significant for solidifying the right first adumbrated in *Eisenstadt*, i.e., a right of sexual autonomy among adults, whether married or unmarried, straight or gay. In this case it was Justice Kennedy who wrote the opinion. Kennedy had been appointed by President Reagan, a Republican, but he assumed the role of a kind of quasi-libertarian on the Court, siding with the conservatives on such issues as limiting federal power while leading the liberals on gay rights cases. Indeed, Kennedy is the author of all of the important decisions protecting gay rights.[101]

Voting to overrule *Bowers* v. *Hardwick* and extend a privacy right, Kennedy wrote for the majority that "adults may choose to enter upon this [sexual] relationship within the confines of their homes and their own private lives and still retain their dignity as free persons."[102] Yet, significantly, while Lawrence trumpets the value of privacy in the lead-up to the decision, the opinion does not use the higher "strict scrutiny" standard reminiscent of *Roe* v. *Wade* and earlier privacy cases. Rather, Justice Kennedy frequently argued simply that statutes affecting gays and lesbians fail to meet the lowest level of scrutiny, rational basis review.[103] The logic is a kind of double-edged sword: on the one hand, *Lawrence* does not elevate protected activities to privacy right protection. On the other hand, they have the effect of disabling state laws prohibiting these activities at the very lowest level – saying, in effect, laws based on morality have no legitimate basis whatsoever.

Indeed, *Lawrence* is the clearest elucidation of the anti-moralistic implications of the privacy right. Justice Kennedy quoted with approval Justice Stevens' dissent in *Bowers* to the effect that, "the fact that the governing majority in a state has traditionally viewed a particular practice as immoral is not a sufficient reason for upholding a law prohibiting the practice."[104] Ultimately, as he concluded, the moral

[100] 539 US 558 (2003).

[101] Justice Kennedy authored *Romer* v. *Evans*, 517 US 620 (1996) (the first case "gay rights" case decided by the Supreme Court. The Court here used the Equal Protection clause to strike down a Colorado constitutional amendment which removed special protection for sexual orientation. Kennedy then authored *Lawrence* v. *Texas*, 539 US 558 (2003) which held unconstitutional laws which prohibited sexual relations among gays, A decade later he wrote the opinion in *United States* v. *Windsor*, 570 US 744 (2013), striking down the federal DOMA act which permitted the federal government to limit Social Security benefits, tax benefits and many other federal benefits to the heterosexual spouses. The final opinion in the series was *Obergefell* v. *Hodges*, 576 US — (2015) holding that the right to marriage cannot be limited to heterosexual couples.

[102] 539 US at 567.

[103] Ibid., at 575.

[104] Ibid., at 577.

disapproval of an activity by the majority does not constitute a "legitimate state interest," the constitutional minimum necessary for a law to be upheld as valid. In sum, there must be some *real harm to third parties* to justify prohibitory legislation.[105]

It is significant to see just how far the Supreme Court has come in respect to morals legislation over the course of the last fifty years. Even as Justice Harlan was asserting a right of married couples to use contraception in his dissent from a denial of the writ of cert in *Poe* v. *Ullman*, he made it abundantly clear that he believed that the "police power" of the state extends to the protection of morality:

> Yet the very inclusion of the category of morality among state concerns indicates that society is not limited in its objects only to the physical well-being of the community, but has traditionally concerned itself with the moral soundness of its people as well. Indeed to attempt a line between public behavior and that which is purely consensual or solitary would be to withdraw from community concern a range of subjects with which every society in civilized times has found it necessary to deal.[106]

By the time of *Lawrence*, even Justice Scalia acknowledged in dissent that the *Lawrence* opinion "effectively decrees the end of all moral legislation."[107] He went on to argue that "[i]f, as the Court asserts, the promotion of majoritarian sexual morality is not even a legitimate state interest, none of the above-mentioned laws [prohibiting fornication, bigamy, adult incest, bestiality and obscenity] can survive rational basis review."[108] Several lower courts have followed this lead, invalidating state bans on fornication and even adultery.[109]

Characteristically, Mill is seldom mentioned directly in these opinions. When he is mentioned at all, it is usually in dissent – when a dissenting justice wants to point out that these decisions come not from the Constitution, but from the realm of political philosophy.[110] The best recent example of this comes from Chief Justice

[105] Ibid., at 578.

[106] *Poe* v. *Ullman*, 367 US at 499.

[107] Ibid., at 599 (Scalia, J., dissenting).

[108] Ibid.

[109] *MacDonald* v. *Moose*, 710 F.3d 154 (2013). *Martin* v. *Ziherl*, 269 Va. 35 (2005). *State* v. *Limon*, 280 Kan. 275 (2005).

[110] See, for example, *State* v. *Erickson*, 574 P.2d 1 (1978), upholding a conviction for possession of cocaine. The concurring, Judge Mathews cites Mill's harm principle at great length in a manner that appear to endorse it while concluding that "thee is responsible authority which indicates that cocaine does sometimes cause anti-social behavior affecting the safety of others." Ibid., at 24–25 (Mathews, J., concurring): *Williams* v. *Attorney General of Alabama*, 378 F.3d 1232 (11th Cir. 2004) (upholding Alabama law prohibiting the sale or use of vibrators, dildos, beads and artificial vaginas). The appellate court held that the position advocated by the district court was "a corollary of John Stuart Mill's celebrated 'harm principle,' which would which would permit the state to allow only conduct that causes identifiable harm to another. [cites omitted]. Regardless of its force as a policy argument, however, it does not translate *ipse dixit* into a constitutionally cognizable standard." Ibid., at 1240. Of course, Mill's principle would have, indeed, embraced the possession of cocaine and sexual devices.

Roberts' dissent in *Obergefell* v. *Hodges*,[111] the case recognizing a constitutional right to gay marriage. In dissent, Roberts responded:

> Then and now, this assertion of the "harm principle" sounds more in philosophy than law. The elevation of the fullest individual self-realization over the constraints that society has expressed in law may or may not be attractive moral philosophy. But a Justice's commission does not confer any special moral, philosophical, or social insight sufficient to justify imposing those perceptions on fellow citizens under the pretense of "due process." There is indeed a process due the people on issues of this sort—the democratic process. Respecting that understanding requires the Court to be guided by law, not any particular school of social thought. As Judge Henry Friendly once put it, echoing Justice Holmes's dissent in *Lochner*, the Fourteenth Amendment does not enact John Stuart Mill's On Liberty any more than it enacts Herbert Spencer's Social Statics.[112]

Of course, it was Justice Kennedy who authored the majority opinion in *Obergefeld* – the same Justice Kennedy who, two decades earlier in the *Casey* case, gave us one of the most striking definitions of liberty in all of Supreme Court jurisprudence:

> At the heart of liberty is the right to define one's own concept of existence, of meaning, of the universe, and of the mystery of human life. Beliefs about these matters could not define the attributes of personhood were they formed under compulsion of the State.[113]

This conception of freedom, which several justices have now accepted as the *elan vital* of the liberty component of the Due Process clause, is pure John Stuart Mill.

111 135 S.Ct. 2584 (2015).

112 Ibid., at 2622.

113 Planned Parenthood of Southwestern *Pennsylvania* v. *Casey*, 505 US 833, 851 (1992). For a discussion of Kennedy's influence, see http://libertymagazine.org/article/justice-kennedys-notorious-mystery-passage.

6

Mill and Modern Freedom of Expression

If Mill is insufficiently credited for the influence he has had on the right to privacy, he is generally acknowledged as one of the premier architects of our modern understanding of freedom of speech. Chapter 2 of *On Liberty*, entitled "Of the Liberty of Thought and Discussion," is widely acknowledged as the single most influential defense of a capaciously generous theory of freedom of speech and press anywhere in modern liberal political thought. No one has influenced the development of modern First Amendment freedom of speech as deeply or as broadly as has Mill.

Theorists usually distinguish between three distinct justifications for freedom of speech and/or press.[1] The most traditional and, arguably, the narrowest rationale views free expression as an important *political* value insofar as free speech is an essential ingredient of self-governance. Democracy requires that a free people have the right to speak on matters of public policy, to criticize their leaders and to petition government for democratic reform. This first "republican" justification for freedom of speech and press was most elegantly defended in recent times by Alexander Meikeljohn.[2]

[1] The Framers themselves seem to have been uncertain about the scope and meaning of free speech. Benjamin Franklin declared that "Few of us, I think, have definite ideas of its nature and extent" and Alexander Hamilton asked "Who can give it any definition that would not leave the utmost latitude for evasion?" Michael I. Meyerson, "The Neglected History of the Prior Restraint Doctrine," 34 *Ind. L. Rev.* 295, 320 (2001).

[2] This rationale, sometimes called the "republican" justification for free speech, was defended most famously by the constitutional theorist, Alexander Meikeljohn *Free Speech and Its Relation to Self-Government* (London: Oxford University Press, 1948). Meikeljohn was explicit in limiting the coverage of freedom of speech. What does the First Amendment protect, he asked? "The town meeting suggests the answer. That meeting is called to discuss [and] to decide matters of public policy.... The first amendment, then, is not the guardian of unrequlated talkativeness. It does not require that, on every occasion, every citizen shall take part in every debate.... When men govern themselves, it is they – and no one else – who must pass judgment on unwisdom and unfairness and danger." Ibid., at 15–16, 24–27.

A second justification conceives of freedom of expression in broader terms as an important *social* value conducive to the truth-finding function of speech. This idea is broader than the first in the sense that it extends free speech protection to social, scientific, cultural, moral and other topics that transcend the narrowly political. It also typically embraces a more adversarial, even Darwinian, notion that permitting the clash of ideas through open discussion and debate is the most efficient way to criticize and discard false notions and opinions and to refine our understanding of the truth.[3]

A third and still more expansive justification holds that freedom of speech serves not only a political, social or public function but a personal, *expressive* function. Where the first two rationales are justified largely in terms of the effect on those who *hear* the message, the third is justified largely for its expressive benefits to the *speaker* himself. According to this theory, expression serves a self-developmental or *individual* autonomy-supporting value by permitting the individual the right to disclose and express his or her innermost feelings and opinions.[4] Another important feature of this third justification is that the right of freedom of expression should protect not simply the rational content of a message but the symbolic, emotional or affective aspects of a message as well.[5]

Mill influenced the development of the First Amendment jurisprudence of the Supreme Court in the twentieth century in three powerfully significant ways. First, he provided the most eloquent and far-reaching defense of the second, truth-finding function of freedom of speech. His theory was the basis for what would later be called the "marketplace of ideas" theory of freedom of speech defended by Justices

3 The "truth-refining" function derives from Mill's thought and, as we will see, influenced Oliver Wendell Holmes Jr.'s "marketplace of ideas" defense of freedom of speech. Following Mill, Holmes argued that diversity of ideas is socially productive in much the same way that a diversity of goods is productive. Ideas should compete for our adherence. See *Abrams* v. *United States*, 250 US 616, 630 (1919) ("when men have realized that time has upset many fighting faiths, they may come to see ... that the ultimate good is better realized by free trade in ideas"). Even false opinions have a value insofar as they help to sharpen our understanding of the truth. And, of course, in matters of politics and morality, what counts as "truth" in the first place is almost always a matter of contention. See infra notes – and text discussing the truth-refining function of freedom of expression.

4 The expressive function is connected with notions of self-respect and self-actualization. As one theorist puts it, "the significance of freedom of expression rests on the central human capacity to create and express symbolic systems, such as speech, writing, pictures and music. Freedom of speech encourages the exercise of these. In so doing, it nurtures and sustains the self-respect of the mature person." David A. J. Richards, "Free Speech and Obscenity: Toward a Moral Theory of the First Amendment," 123 *U. Pa. L. Rev.* 45, 62 (1974).

5 In *Cohen* v. *California*, for example, the Court relied on just such an emotive or expressive idea of speech in holding that the First Amendment protects a man to walk into a courthouse with a T-shirt that says, "F— the draft." The prosecution argued that he could have expressed the rational content of the message in various ways but that the form of expression violated laws prohibiting foul speech in a public place. The Court ruled, however, that the language was part of the message and was, thus, protected.

Holmes and Brandeis, among others. In sum, Mill deepened our understanding of the underlying *justification* for free speech.

Second, Mill's harm principle also had implications for the permissible *limits* of free speech rights. Applying the harm principle to free speech had the effect of broadening its protection and providing, in effect, that the state cannot limit speech that does not rise to the level of true harm, i.e., "offensive" speech or forms of expression deemed to be immoral.

Third, Mill began to lay the groundwork for the expressive justification for free speech. He connected the expressive function with his underlying understanding of liberty as self-individuation, demonstrating how speech acts can be constitutive of personal autonomy and self-development. He also suggested that it was dangerous to attempt to separate the rational or propositional aspects of a message from its emotional or affective content – that censorship of *the way* in which a thing is expressed often amounts to censorship of the propositional content of the message.

In each of these ways, Mill was the prophet of the greatly expanded free speech protection of the Supreme Court of the 1960s and beyond.

MILL'S THEORY OF FREEDOM OF THOUGHT AND DISCUSSION

Freedom of expression is one of three core liberal values in Mill's understanding of liberty, along with the right of privacy and equality. Privacy is necessary to the right of self-development and equality ensures that each individual has basically the same opportunities to develop themselves – but expression, in a sense, is the fullest outworking of the still more interior domain of freedom of thought, which is nurtured by the privacy right.

Freedom of expression was, for Mill, not simply one among other liberties. Rather, expression is tied to the core purpose of liberty *simpliciter.* The relationship between free thought and free expression is intimate and reciprocal. Any meaningful conception of freedom of expression obviously depends on freedom to think one's own thoughts: one must have *something to say* of *one's own* to make the liberty of expressing that thought a meaningful act. But, less obviously, the reverse is true as well. If we are not free to express what we think – if we are threatened or sanctioned for uttering out loud what we believe to be true in the depths of our hearts – then these thoughts themselves, closeted away in the recesses of our minds, are destined to atrophy. At the end of the day, prohibiting certain forms of expression discourages certain forms of thought which, in turn, is an insidious if indirect way of controlling not only what the individual *thinks*, but *who he becomes*.

Mill makes this connection between expression and self-development in various places in *On Liberty*. Recall that the very first freedom in Mill's tripartite taxonomy of our most essential liberties, which he outlined in Chapter 1, was "liberty of conscience in the most comprehensive sense." This inner freedom of conscience includes the "absolute freedom of opinion and sentiment on all subjects, practical or speculative, scientific, moral and theological."[6] And this freedom of opinion embraces, in turn, an *unlimited freedom* of "expressing and publishing [these] opinions" since the right to publish an opinion is "practically inseparable" from liberty of thought.[7]

At another point, Mill observed that certain forms of indirect social tyranny can be "more formidable than many forms of political oppression" precisely because they "leave[] fewer means of escape, penetrating much more deeply into the details of life and enslaving the soul itself."[8] In sum, freedom of expression is both a completion of, and a necessary condition of, the freedom of development which falls at the heart of liberty.

Just as freedom of expression completes the inward quest for self-development, it is connected, in turn, to the outward pursuit of truth and social progress. Chapter 2 of *On Liberty* focuses on the "truth-finding" function of speech necessary to these latter ends.

Mill's basic objective was to defend the fullest expression of beliefs and opinions, whether or not a particular opinion is thought to be true or false. No idea may be censored and no opinion proscribed because of its content, because of the majority's view that it may be false or even dangerous. First, the proscribed opinion might turn out to be true in which case censoring it will be detrimental to our understanding of truth, of reality, of the way the world works. Thus, the lone dissenter must never be silenced for he may turn out to have the correct understanding of truth:

> If all mankind minus one were of one opinion, mankind would be no more justified in silencing that one person than he, if he had the power, would be justified in silencing mankind ... [T]he peculiar evil of silencing the expression of an opinion is that it is robbing the human race, posterity as well as the existing generation – those who dissent from it still more than those who hold it.[9]

Yet even if the opinion is rightly believed to be false, there are two reasons against censoring it. First, a false opinion might still have a grain of truth within it. In his own personal "transition" in which Mill turned over every new intellectual influence to discover what was true in it, and what was false, he became convinced that "truth" is often complex, many-sided and variegated.[10] True understanding requires looking at a subject from all sides, listening to every opinion and weighing it against contrary opinion." The only way a human being can make the approach

[6] John Stuart Mill, *On Liberty*, *CW*, 18:225.

[7] Ibid.

[8] Mill, *On Liberty*, 18:219–20. Mill's passion swells in passages such as this, where he is warning of the "tyranny of the majority." Indeed, Mill had imbibed his Tocqueville, who coined that phrase. (Tocqueville, in fact, died the year *On Liberty* was published.)

[9] Ibid., 229.

[10] Truth, in the great practical concerns of life, is so much a question of the reconciling and combing of opposites that very few have minds sufficiently capacious and impartial to make the adjustment with an approach to correctness, and it has to be made in the rough process of a struggle between combatants fighting under hostile banners." Ibid., at 254.

to knowing the whole of a subject is by hearing what can be said about it by persons of every variety of opinion, and studying all modes by which it can be looked at by every character of mind."[11]

The "many-sidedness" of truth was particularly significant in the spheres of politics, morality and economics, where principles have a practical rather than an absolute character. Not surprisingly, censorship is most often practiced in these very spheres. Mill drew largely the same distinction, with the same import, as Aristotle: political and ethical truths are understood through *phronesis*, or practical wisdom, not *sophia*, or theoretical knowledge. As such, they require the exercise of judgment, nuance, equity and perspective – an exercise which depends on the openness of discussion and debate. Mill mentioned as an example here his own belief that free markets are the best economic policy "nineteen times out of twenty." But because even this principle is a practical truth, it needs to be qualified and will have exceptions.[12] This refinement and qualification of our understanding requires dialectical debate. Thus, freedom of expression permits this gradual refinement of our understanding of an issue by permitting us to hear answers on all sides of a question.

The second reason for protecting even a putatively false opinion is the effect upon the character of public debate and, indeed, on the depth of understanding of those who hold the presumptively true opinion. Mill rightly insisted that our grasp of the truth is refined and enlivened by its clash with false ideas. Censorship is always corrosive of the truth even if the censored opinion is false: "If the opinion is right, [we] are deprived of the opportunity of exchanging error for truth; if wrong, [we] lose what is almost as great a benefit: the clearer perception and livelier impression of truth produced by its collision with error."[13]

One of Mill's most profound psychological insights has to do with the effects of censorship on those who hold even presumptively "true" opinions. When insulated from debate, these generally accepted truths tend to deteriorate into dull platitudes that no longer excite our imagination or nurture our deeper understanding of them:

> But when [some opinion or view] has come to be an hereditary creed, and to be received passively, not actively – when the mind is no longer compelled, in the same degree as at first... there is a progressive tendency to forget all of the belief except the formularies, or to give it a dull and torpid assent, as if accepting it on trust dispensed with the necessity of realizing it in consciousness, or testing it by personal experience, until it almost ceases to connect itself at all with the inner life of the human being.[14]

[11] Ibid., at 232.

[12] Believing with Mr. Comte that there are no absolute truths in the political art... we agree with him that the laissez faire doctrine, stated without large qualifications, is both unpractical and unscientific, but it does not follow that those who assert it are not, nineteen times out of twenty, practically nearer the truth than those who deny it." Ibid., at 303.

[13] Ibid., at 229.

[14] Ibid., at 248.

Stifling freedom of speech thus has a doubly disabling affect. In the absence of vigorous discussion and debate, even true doctrines deteriorate into passively held "prejudices with little comprehension or feeling of its rational grounds."[15] Where opinions are not challenged and defended, moreover, people no longer appreciate what the doctrine *really means*.

Worse still, this has a degenerative effect not only on the doctrines themselves but on the "conduct and character" of those who passively hold them. Here, again, Mill drew the connection between freedom and the development of the inner self. Where beliefs and opinions are no longer debated, even their defenders are deprived "of any real or heartfelt conviction from reason or personal experience."[16] This impoverishes the individual in the closest way to which Mill could call "spiritual." What it means to be a fully realized human being is to hold views which one has examined for himself, not simply to accept them because they have been learned at the knee of the parent or the professor.[17] This is, again, the problem with custom, habit and tradition for Mill: they rob the individual of forming a genuine understanding even of those traditional truths worth preserving.[18]

Mill's encomia enthusiastically praising the progressive unfolding of truth were not based on some romanticized notion that truth magically wins out in the clash of ideas.[19] He was an empiricist, after all, and his belief in the progress of truth is almost inseparable from his skepticism. His was a sober faith that freedom of thought and discussion could gradually eliminate false opinion, prejudice and superstition over the long haul.[20] That freedom and diversity of ideas is essential to this process was central to his progressivism. Again, his was not an inevitable Hegelian progressivism, but a progressivism born of the hard-won fight for truth in the real world, the empirical world.

[15] Ibid., at 258.

[16] Ibid.

[17] As he wrote in an early essay, "To have erroneous conviction is one evil but to have no strong or deep-seated convictions at all is an enormous one. Before I compliment either a man or a generation upon having gotten rid of their prejudices, I require to know what they have substituted in lieu of them." John Stuart Mill, *Spirit of the Age*, CW, 22:233.

[18] One is reminded of Thomas Jefferson's skepticism about tradition and the Constitution:

> {Some] men look at constitutions with sanctimonious reverence and deem them, like the Ark of the Covenant, too sacred to be touched. They ascribe to the men of the preceding age a wisdom more than human, and suppose what they did to be beyond amendment. I knew that age well. {it] was like the present, but without the experience of the present. Let us not weakly believe that one generation is not as capable as another of taking care of itself, and of ordering its own affairs.... The dead have no rights.

Thomas Jefferson, Letter to Samuel Kercheval, July 12, 1816, *The Portable Thomas Jefferson* (New York: Penguin Books, 1977), 558–59.

[19] "It is an piece of idle sentimentality that truth, merely as truth, has any inherent power denied to error of prevailing against the dungeon and the stake." Mill, *On Liberty*, CW, 18:238.

[20] "Wrong opinion and practices gradually yield to fact and argument, but facts and arguments, to produce any effect on the mind, must be brought before it." Ibid., at 231. Yet, "the dictum that truth always triumphs over persecution is one of those pleasant falsehoods which men repeat one after the other, till they pass into commonplaces, but which all experience refutes." Ibid., 238.

Mill set only one limit on the right to free speech – a limit which is a corollary of the harm principle. Just as the state should not prohibit *conduct* unless it directly harms another, so too, "even opinions lose their immunity when the circumstances in which they are expressed are such as to constitute … a positive instigation to some mischievous act."[21] Mill's example of this "clear and present danger" test makes abundantly clear how broad a principle it is:

> An opinion that corn dealers are starvers of the poor, or that private property is robbery ought to be unmolested when simply circulated through the press, but may justly incur punishment when delivered orally to an excited mob assembled before the house of a corn dealer, or when handed about in the same mob in the form of a placard.[22]

Nothing but an incitement to direct violence should be sufficient to silence an opinion.

Mill's understanding of the legitimate limits of free speech soon influenced Oliver Wendell Holmes, Jr. and Louis Brandeis in their famous First Amendment dissents after World War I.

HOLMES, BRANDEIS AND THE DEVELOPMENT OF THE CLEAR AND PRESENT DANGER TEST

Recall from our discussion in Chapter 4 that there was very little in the way of any fundamental rights protections during the first "republican" constitutional era. Only after the ratification of the Fourteenth Amendment in 1868 did the Supreme Court begin to think more systematically about the foundations and meaning of some of our most important rights, including freedom of speech. This was precisely the period when the ideas Mill had defended in *On Liberty*, first published in 1859, began to spread and to influence thinkers of the next generation.

Oliver Wendell Holmes, Jr. and Louis D. Brandeis were undoubtedly the two most influential Supreme Court justices during the first third of the twentieth century, the period when the Court began to think systematically about the nature of individual rights. Neither found attractive the Lochner era/Due Process protection for economic liberties. On the other hand, both Holmes and Brandeis were the two most directly influenced by Mill. Both were considerably more than judges who happened to ascend to the highest level of the American judiciary. Each was a bona fide thinker in his own right. Both had read widely and thought deeply about

[21] Ibid., at 260.

[22] Ibid., K. C. O'Rourke, *John Stuart Mill and Freedom of Expression* (2001), 126–27. Mill placed the line here because he thought that enciting others to violence represents the line between speech and harmful action.

the political and social issues of their time. Both grew up surrounded by books in homes where broad reading of philosophy, history and literature were strongly encouraged. Both were at the forefront of the emerging movement of legal realism – the twentieth-century's response to the formalism of the nineteenth century.

We saw in the last chapter that Brandeis was intimately familiar with Mill's ideas. As for Holmes, he was born in 1841, two years before the first of Mill's important works, A *System of Logic*, appeared. Under the tutelage of his father, the poet, Oliver Wendell Holmes, Sr., and such learned friends of the Holmes family as Ralph Waldo Emerson, Holmes had read widely in philosophy, history and political thought.[23] He read both James Mill's, *The Analysis of the Phenomena of the Mind*, which provided a materialist and associational theory of psychology, and J. S. Mill's *System of Logic*, while still in his teens.[24] The latter work, in particular, would have been incredibly heavy sledding for a neophyte but its skeptical influence is apparent in much of Holmes' later philosophy. His famous dictum in defense of legal realism that "the life of the law has not been logic: it has been experience"[25] could have been lifted directly from the pages of the *System of Logic*, which had advanced a highly inductive form of reasoning inimical to the claims of deductive or a priori truths. And not only had Holmes read *On Liberty*, one early biographer reported that he knew both *On Liberty* and *Utilitarianism* practically by heart.[26]

Mill's name appears almost a dozen times in Holmes' correspondence with Harold Laski. In one letter, he compared Carlyle to Mill:

> Carlyle's thoughts were rooted in his temperament, his prejudices and his imagination. Mill's were detached by reason. People pay higher for luxuries than for necessaries, and Carlyle's pictures may outlast Mill's thoughts but I doubt if Carlyle gave the world as great a shove as Mill.[27]

But Mill's influence on Holmes was even more direct and personal than that gleaned from reading the master as a youth. In fact, Holmes met Mill and spent several days with him in 1866. Holmes had recently returned home from the Civil War, where he had nearly given his life in service to the North. Now back home, his father arranged a visit to England through their friend, Leslie Stephen. After Holmes had arrived in London, Mill invited Holmes to dinner at the Political

[23] Catherine Drinker Bowen, *Yankee from Olympus: Justice Holmes and His Family* (Boston: Little Brown and Company, 1944).

[24] Ibid., 187.

[25] O. W. Holmes, Jr., *Common Law* (Boston: Little, Brown and Company, 1881), 1.

[26] Bowen, *Yankee from Olympus*, 228.

[27] O. W. Holmes and Harold J. Laski, *Holmes–Laski Letters*, ed. Mark de Witt Howe, Vol. 2, 1926–1935 (Boston: Harvard University Press, 1953), 117 (Letter of November 1, 1926).

Economy Club, a London venue for political debate established by James Mill in the 1820s. At each of these dinners, a topic was assigned for discussion. The subject of the discussion for that evening was whether the financial policy of England should be modified to meet the predicted exhaustion of coal resources in ninety years.[28]

Holmes reached the Supreme Court in 1902 and Brandeis, the first Jewish justice, in 1916. With the backdrop of the Communist Revolution in Russia in 1917 and the end of World War I a year later, the stage was set for the Court to begin to develop the constitutional jurisprudence of free speech in the years immediately afterward.

As we saw in the privacy rights context, even those justices influenced by the Millian interpretation of liberty did not leap straightaway from the status quo to a rigorous adherence to Mill's ideas. And so it was with freedom of speech. The traditional limit on freedom of speech was known as the "bad tendency" test. The bad tendency test was the free speech equivalent of morals legislation in the privacy context: speech could be restrained, or punished after the fact, if the speech had the natural and reasonable tendency to promote bad acts (i.e., illegal conduct or conduct deemed inimical to public welfare).[29] But in 1919, with the first important free speech cases now before the Court, Holmes offered a different test gleaned from Mill.

In *Schenk* v. *United States*[30] the defendant was convicted under the Espionage Act of 1917 for distributing literature urging draftees to resist induction into the armed forces. Holmes wrote for a unanimous court in upholding Schenk's conviction while introducing the "clear and present danger" test:

> The most stringent protection of free speech would not protect a man in falsely shouting fire in a theatre and causing a panic. ... The question in every case is whether the words used are used in such circumstances and are of such a nature as to create a clear and present danger that they will bring about the substantive evils that Congress has a right to prevent. It is a question of proximity and degree.[31]

Although the new test was intended to liberalize the standard – to prevent prosecution for a person's beliefs and ideas – in this case Holmes wrote to uphold the conviction. He argued that "when a nation is at war, many things that might be said

[28] Nicholas Capaldi, *John Stuart Mill: A Life* (Cambridge: Cambridge University Press, 2004), 351.

[29] *Patterson* v. *Colorado*, 205 US 454 (1907), where the Court adopted the bad tendency test from the English common law. See David Rabban, "Clear and Present Danger Test," in *Oxford Companion to the Supreme Court of the United States*, eds. Kermit L. Hall, Joel B. Grossman and James W. Ely (New York: Oxford University Press, 2005), 183.

[30] 249 US 47 (1919).

[31] 249 US at 55.

in time of peace are such a hindrance to its effort that their utterance will not be endured so long as men fight, and that no Court could regard them as protected by any constitutional right."[32] A week later, Holmes used the same test to uphold the convictions in two other high-profile cases, one including the leader of the Socialist party, Eugene Debs.[33]

These cases were decided in the spring, 1919. But with the new term, which began in the fall of the same year, Holmes began to use a more aggressive version of the test – in defense of a broader conception of freedom of speech. The case that came before the Court in that term was *Abrams* v. *United States*.[34] Though the Court's majority upheld Abrams' conviction under the same Espionage Act used in the earlier cases. Holmes and Brandeis dissented. Holmes, who wrote the dissent, argued that the defendants here did not pose the same clear and present danger as the defendants had in *Schenk*, *Frohwerk* and *Debs*. Circumstances mattered, and by this time, the threat of obstructing the war effort had passed. The incitement, moreover, had been more indirect, diffused. Abrams had thrown leaflets from a New York City window, some in Yiddish, denouncing the decision to send troops to impede the Russian Revolution and advocating a strike on the production of munitions. This did not amount to a genuine "clear and present danger."

Holmes charged in his dissent that the "defendants are to be made to suffer not for what the indictment alleges, but for the creed that they avow."[35] It was here that he offered one of the most eloquent, if sardonic, defenses of free speech ever:

> Prosecution for the expression of opinions seems to me perfectly logical. If you have no doubt of your premises or your power and want a certain result with all your heart you naturally express your wishes in law and sweep away all opposition. To allow opposition to speech seems to indicate that you think the speech impotent. … But when men have realized that time has upset many fighting faiths, they may come to believe even more than they believe the very foundations of their own conduct that the ultimate good desired is better reached by free trade in ideas – that the best test of truth is the power to get itself accepted in the competition of the market. … That, at any rate, is the theory of our Constitution. It is an experiment, as all life is an experiment.[36]

All of this – the appeal to the competition of "fighting faiths," the sense that evolution is best served by "the free trade in ideas" and the idea that "all life is an experiment" – are pure John Stuart Mill. And just as Brandeis had reread Mill

[32] Ibid., at 56.
[33] *Frohwerk* v. *United States*, 249 US 204 (1919); *Debs* v. *United States*, 249 US 211 (1919).
[34] 250 US 616 (1919).
[35] 250 US at 629 (Holmes, J., dissenting).
[36] Abrams, 250 US at 630 (Holmes, J., dissenting).

before his *Olmstead* dissent, scholars have suggested that Holmes had recently reread his *On Liberty* shortly before the Abrams decision, and that this had galvanized Holmes' convictions in the direction of greater protection for free speech.[37]

Holmes and Brandeis dissented again in 1925, in *Gitlow* v. *New York*.[38] Gitlow had arranged for the publication of a manifesto representing the views of the "left wing" of the socialist party in its official periodical, *The Revolutionary Age*. Though the Court conceded that the publication had had no material consequences – that defendant had not convinced anyone to break the law – he was convicted for *advocating* the overthrow of the US government. Holmes, again joined by Brandeis, used language almost identical to Mill's that "[t]he question in each case is whether the words used are used in such circumstances and are of such a nature as to create a clear and present danger that they will bring about the substantive evils that the state has a right to prevent."[39] In this case, as in Abrams, the answer was "no." The publication had been an inconsequential publication put out by a small band of radicals with no material effect upon anyone. To the argument that the manifesto was intended to incite others to break the law, Holmes responded:

> Every idea is an incitement. It offers itself for belief and, if believed, it is acted on unless some other belief outweighs it, or some failure of energy stifles the movement at its birth. The only difference between the expression of an opinion and an incitement in the narrower sense is the speaker's enthusiasm for the result. Eloquence may set fire to reason. … If, in the long run, the beliefs expressed in proletarian dictatorship are destined to be accepted by the dominant forces of the community, the only meaning of free speech is that they should be given that chance and have their way.[40]

Two years later, in *Whitney* v. *California*,[41] the Court was faced with the conviction of a woman not for unlawful action, or even speech, but for *membership* in a radical organization. Whitney was convicted under the California Criminal Syndicalism Act, which prohibited anyone from knowingly being a member of any organization which advocated the use of crime, sabotage or terrorism to effect political change, or

37 Richard Polenberg, *Fighting Faiths: The Abrams Case, the Supreme Court and Free Speech* (Cornell: Cornell University Press, 1987), 217–18; Scholars have suggested that his change in views were the product of a lively exchange the previous summer between he and two other important legal theorists, Harold Laski and Judge Learned Hand, among others, David M. Rabban, "The Emergence of Modern First Amendment Doctrine," 50 *U. Chi. L. Rev.* 1207, 1311–17 (1983) (discussing this exchange).

38 268 US 652 (1925).

39 268 US at 652 (Holmes, J., dissenting). Holmes' language echoes Mill's in the corn dealer example.

40 *Gitlow* v. *New York*, 268 US 252 (1925) (Holmes, J., dissenting).

41 274 US 357 (1927).

a change in the ownership of industry. Though Whitney had testified that she had opposed change through violence, the Court upheld her conviction, arguing that membership in an organization which represents a clear threat to the public peace was even more dangerous than the "isolated utterances" of others who had defended radical causes.

Justice Brandeis (joined in his opinion by Holmes), concurred in the judgment insofar as counsel for defendant had not raised any free speech claims. But he attacked the core of the Court's reasoning, pointing out that the Court had not yet set the standard for how "clear" and "present" the danger must be – "how remote the danger may be and yet be deemed present, and what degree of evil shall be deemed sufficiently substantial."[42] Then, echoing Mill's assertion that "If all mankind minus one were of one opinion, mankind would be no more justified in silencing that one person than he, if he had the power, would be justified in silencing mankind," Brandeis asserted that we must "bear in mind why a state is, ordinarily, denied the power to prohibit the dissemination of social, economic and political doctrine a vast majority of its citizens believes to be false and fraught with evil consequences."[43] The Framers of the First Amendment "believ[ed] in the power of reason as applied through public discussion, they eschewed silence coerced by law."[44] Brandeis then wove together several of the various strands of Mill's argument from *On Liberty* – the progressive realization of truth and elimination of falsehood afforded by freedom of speech, the connection between freedom of thought and freedom of discussion, the appeal to liberty as the primary means of individual self-development and, finally, the idea that freedom is most threatened by the blind acceptance of "hereditary creeds" by an inert polity:

> Those who won our independence believed that the final end of the state was to make men free to develop their faculties and that in its government, the deliberative forces should prevail over the arbitrary. They valued liberty both as an end and as a means. They believed liberty to be the secret of happiness and courage to be the secret of liberty. They believed that freedom to think as you will and to speak as you think are means indispensable to the discovery and spread of political truth ... discussion affords ordinarily adequate protection against the dissemination of noxious doctrine, that the greatest menace to freedom is an inert people ...[45]

Both the spirit and the substance of this argument were drawn from Mill.

As developed by the Supreme Court, the "clear and present danger" test never quite embodied the standard Mill set out in his corn dealer example, though some of Holmes' and Brandeis' language at times approached it. The standard was eviscerated in still later rulings, however, when the Court purported to use it while according

[42] Ibid., at 375 (Brandeis, J., concurring).
[43] Ibid.
[44] Ibid., at 377.
[45] Ibid.

even less protection to freedom of speech. In *Dennis* v. *United States*,[46] decided in 1951, well after Holmes and Brandeis were gone and at the height of the "Red Scare," the Court upheld the conviction under the Smith Act of several defendants who had been organizers of the Communist Party and/or had advocated Marxist-Leninist doctrines. In upholding the convictions, the majority purported to adopt the clear and present danger test, but in fact adopted a balancing test developed by Judge Learned Hand in which the probability and extent of the evil (overthrow of the government) was balanced against the liberty of freedom of speech.[47] Justice Jackson concurred, writing that he would reserve the use of the test for a case (similar to Mill's corn dealer example) involving a "hot-headed speech on a street corner."[48]

Justice Douglas, who was to become the new torchbearer for free speech, dissented in *Dennis*. He argued that defendants had been convicted for teaching Marxist-Leninist doctrines and nothing more. The Court had disregarded the lines between teaching and advocacy, and advocacy and incitement, Douglas argued. Given that books such as the Communist Manifesto were available at any bookstore and could be discussed and debated openly, what made this a crime, Douglas charged, was not "what is said, but [] the intent with which it is said. Once we start down that road we enter territory dangerous to the liberties of every citizen."[49]

Appointed to the Court by FDR in 1939, a few years after Holmes and Brandeis retired, Justice Douglas represented the next generation of justices who had imbibed deeply of the spirit of John Stuart Mill. On the civil liberties side, Douglas was probably the most libertarian justice of all time. He quoted or paraphrased Mill frequently in his speeches and opinions including, as we saw in the last chapter, his privacy opinions in *Poe* v. *Ullman* and *Doe* v. *Bolton*. In his book *Anatomy of Liberty: The Rights of Man without Force*, Justice Douglas presented a broadly Millian interpretation of the American constitution, at one point comparing Mill with Thomas Jefferson:

> Jefferson's theory and the idea espoused by the Britisher, John Stuart Mill, have common ground. Mill wrote, 'If all mankind minus one, were of one opinion, and only one person were of the contrary opinion, mankind would be no more justified in silencing that one person, than he, if he had the power, would be justified in silencing mankind.'[50]

[46] 341 US 494 (1951).

[47] Judge Hand had advanced the same utilitarian formula in various contexts, including tort law. See *United States* v. *Carroll Towing*, 160 F.2d 482 (Second Cir., 1945). Hand had been the lower court appellate judge in the Dennis case, and had advocated the balancing test for almost thirty years, but his test protected less than the more rigorous use to which it was put by Holmes and Brandeis.

[48] 341 US at 568.

[49] Ibid., at 589.

[50] William O. Douglas, *The Anatomy of Liberty: The Rights of Man without Force* (New York: Simon and Schuster, 1963), 8.

He wrote this in 1963 – just two years before his privacy right decision in Griswold and six years before Douglas's concurring opinion in *Brandenburg* v. *Ohio*,[51] which finally enshrined the substance of Mill's theory of freedom of expression.

Brandenburg, a Ku Klux Klan member, was convicted under Ohio's criminal syndicalism statute after he was filmed at a KKK rally burning a cross, brandishing weapons and giving a speech in which he declared, among other things, that "if our President, our Congress, our Supreme Court, continues to suppress the white, Caucasian race, it's possible that there might have to be some revengerance [sic] taken."[52] In a *per curium* opinion, the Court reversed the conviction and set forth a new standard: speech can only be punished when it is an incitement to "imminent lawless action."[53] This embodied what Mill had conveyed in his example of the speech involving the corn dealer. Speech can only be restricted or restrained when it is likely to produce an imminent threat of harm to third parties. Justice Douglas wrote a concurring opinion in which he arguably went further:

> The line between what is permissible and not subject to control and what may be made impermissible and subject to regulation is the line between ideas and overt acts. The example usually given by those who would punish speech is the case of one who falsely shouts fire in a crowded theatre ... a case where speech is brigaded with action. ... Apart from rare instances of that kind, speech is, I think, immune from prosecution.[54]

By Douglas's reasoning, even Holmes and Brandeis had not gone far enough insofar as they were willing to weigh the threat of public consequences against the right to speak. Indeed, where Holmes and Judge Learned Hand had at times advocated a kind of utilitarian standard by which speech could be balanced against the threat of public harm, Douglas followed Mill in advocating something well beyond this limit: speech could not be punished unless it was "brigaded with action," i.e., so intertwined with action that is was likely to cause direct, harmful consequences such that it amounts to action itself.

SPEECH AND THE HARM PRINCIPLE: OFFENSIVE AND IMMORAL SPEECH

The "imminent lawless action" standard was perhaps the most significant way in which the Supreme Court imported Mill's harm principle into the domain of political speech where restrictions were based on the putative *dangerousness* of

[51] 395 US 444 (1969). Brandenburg, a Ku Klux Klan member, was convicted under Ohio's criminal syndicalism statute for advocating violence at a Klan rally. In a *per curium* opinion, the Court reversed his conviction holding that political speech receives the highest form of protection under the Constitution, and that a person may not be punished for speech unless he intentionally is inciting others to imminent lawless action, similar to Mill's corn dealer example.

[52] 395 US at 346.

[53] Ibid.

[54] Ibid., at 355.

the speech. But in a series of decisions beginning well before *Brandenburg*, the Supreme Court and other lower courts began working their way toward other applications of the harm principle in the sphere of free speech. Most important among these involved cases challenging the myriad regulations based on the offensiveness or putative immorality of certain forms of speech. Mill had argued that speech, like action, could not be punished or restrained because it is thought to be offensive. Beginning in the 1940s, the Court began to move toward a similar understanding.

One of the first areas in which the Court began to reexamine the common law limits on free speech involved abusive or provocative speech. In *Cantwell* v. *Connecticut*, decided in 1940, the Supreme Court overturned the conviction of a Jehovah's Witness who had stopped passers-by to ask if they would listen to a phonograph recording in which Roman Catholicism and other organized religions were attacked as instruments of Satan.[55] While several listeners were highly offended and one even contemplated attacking Cantwell, the Court emphasized that the recordings did not contain profane, indecent or abusive language directed at the listeners. The Court held ultimately that the offensive character of the speech was not a sufficient basis to justify its prohibition, particularly since Cantwell's speech was not directed toward the listeners in a personal sense.

A few years later, in 1949, the Court expanded the principle by covering *deliberately and directly* offensive and provocative speech. *Terminello* v. *Chicago*, another opinion by Justice Douglas, concerned a speech given by a suspended Catholic priest, who had deliberately appropriated the style of European fascist leaders. Terminello insulted various racial and ethnic groups and taunted his audience, calling them "snakes," "slimy scum" and "bedbugs."[56] In reversing the conviction for disturbing the peace, Douglas declared that "the function of free speech under our system is to invite dispute"[57]

This same principle received its most fulsome protection by the Illinois Supreme Court in 1978 in *Skokie* v. *National Socialist Party of America*. The Illinois Nazi Party planned to display a swastika and to march (rather than giving a speech in a segregated area) down the streets of Skokie, Illinois, a Chicago suburb. The town had been chosen specifically because many Jewish survivors of the Holocaust lived there.[58] The Village of Skokie had argued that the purposes of free speech could be served by permitting the Nazis to speak in other places and that seeing the swastika

55 310 US 296 (1940).

56 337 US 1 (1949).

57 Ibid., at 10. But see *Feiner* v. *New York*, 340 US 315 (1951), upholding the arrest of a speaker who continued to speak as a crown grew unruly. The speech was on a street corner and the sole policeman stopped him only after he had spoken for thirty minutes as the crowd closed in around the speaker and the policeman. The Court found that there was a "clear and present danger" of a riot erupting; *Chaplinksy* v. *New Hampshire*, 315 US 568 (1942) ("fighting words" exception to free speech).

58 *Village of Skokie* v. *National Socialist Party of America*, 373 N.E.2d 21 (IL. 1978).

would be like being physically assaulted for those who had endured the Holocaust. They insisted that even political speech, which is most highly protected under the First Amendment, does not embrace a general right of the speaker to speak wherever he wishes, and to do so for the sole purpose of causing offense. But the Illinois Supreme Court rejected these arguments, holding that speech cannot be curtailed because of its offensive character.[59]

Another aspect of the harm principle, as we saw in the previous chapter, is that action may not be curtailed on the basis of the putative *immorality* of the act, the example it may create or the tendency it may induce in others. Similarly, the anti-moralistic implications of the harm principle entail that speech may not be censored or punished simply because it is considered lewd, profane or sexually provocative. The common law test for obscenity permitted prosecution whenever "the tendency of the matter is [to] deprive and corrupt those whose minds are open to such immoral influences."[60] This paralleled the common law defense of morals legislation in the sphere of activity. Slowly, during the same period when the Supreme Court began to develop the constitutional right to privacy, it began to erode this common law test, narrowing the permissible grounds for state regulation of allegedly obscene material.

In the 1973 case of *Miller* v. *California*, the Court modified the earlier tests for obscenity. It held that the determination as to what counts as "obscene" should be made according to contemporary community standards.[61] Though this did not create absolute protection for pornography, it meant that juries could – and increasingly did – relax the standard for obscenity. In other cases, the Court found other grounds for invalidating overly restrictive ordinances regulating adult content in drive-ins and movie theaters.[62] In some of these cases, Mill's influence was candidly acknowledged, even when the Court stopped short of fully embracing his principles. In a companion case to *Miller*, *Paris Adult Theatre I* v. *Slayton*, for example, the Court upheld an injunction against the showing of pornographic films in an adult theater in Atlanta, Georgia.[63] Citing *On Liberty*, the majority opinion, written by the conservative Chief justice Burger, asserted "for us to say that our Constitution incorporates the proposition that conduct involving consenting adults only is always beyond state regulation – is a step we are unable to take."[64]

59 See Lee Bollinger and Aryeh Neier, "The Skokie Legacy: Reflections on an 'Easy Case' and Free Speech Theory," 80 *Michigan Law Review* 617 (1982).

60 *Regina* v. *Hicklin*, 31 R.Q.B.360, 371 (1868).

61 413 US 15 (1973).

62 See, for example, *Erznoznik* v. *Jacksonville*, 422 US 205 (1975) (invalidating local ordinance that prohibited drive in theaters that were visible from the street from showing movies portraying nude buttocks, female breasts or adult public areas).

63 413 US 49 (1973).

64 413 US at 68, n. 14, citing Mill's *On Liberty*.

In the context of prosecutions for broadcasting profanity, as opposed to obscenity, courts also frequently found ways to narrow the scope of regulation in the context of broadcasting. In *FCC* v. *Pacifica Foundation*, for example, the Supreme Court upheld the FCC sanction of a radio station's broadcast of George Carlin's "Seven Words You Can't Say on Television" but allowed that such broadcasts could take place at appropriate hours – at times when younger listeners would be asleep.[65]

Yet the Court was willing to go much further in the direction of free speech when allegedly profane speech was more localized (i.e., not the subject of a radio or TV broadcast). In *Cohen* v. *California*, it overturned the conviction for disturbing the peace of a man who wore a T-shirt with the words "Fuck the Draft!" into a California courthouse. The opinion, authored by Justice Harlan, declared that

> [G]overnment bodies may not prescribe the form or content of individual expression. While the particular four-letter word is perhaps more distasteful than most others of its genre, it is nevertheless true that one man's vulgarity is another man's lyric.[66]

The opinion went on to reject the traditional line between the rational substance of a speech act and its affective or emotional content:

> [L]inguistic expression serves a dual communicative function: it conveys ideas not only capable of relatively precise, detached explication but otherwise inexpressible emotions as well. We cannot sanction the view that the Constitution, while solicitous of the cognitive content of individual speech, has little or no regard for that emotive function which, practically speaking, may often be the more important element of the overall message.[67]

Indeed, the government had tried to argue that *Cohen* could have conveyed the substance of his political message in a more neutral, or less offensive, manner. The Court responded that it is not possible to prohibit one without the other.

> We cannot indulge the facile assumption that one can forbid particular words without also running a substantial risk of suppressing ideas in the process. Indeed, government might seize on the censorship of particular words as a convenient guise for banning the expression of unpopular views.[68]

These ideas – that heartfelt emotion breathes life into persuasion, that the very act of expressing both the rational and the emotive aspects of a message has a beneficial effect on speaker and hearer alike and that, without the emotional edge provided by free and open debate, our positions lose their flavor and force so that understanding itself suffers – all reflect the legacy of Mill's libertarian romanticism.

[65] 438 US 726 (1978).
[66] 403 US at 22.
[67] Ibid., at 23.
[68] Ibid.

"BREATHING SPACE" FOR FREE SPEECH: PROTECTION FOR FALSE STATEMENTS OF FACT

Mill's defense of freedom of speech embraced the freedom to defend beliefs, ideas, opinions or facts that might turn out to be false. He adduced three reasons for this: First, the putatively false idea may turn out to be true. Censoring an idea on the basis of its alleged falsehood often means censoring ideas that are later found to be true. Second, even if the idea is false, it may be more difficult than we might imagine to separate the wheat from the chaff. False claims may contain (more than) a grain of truth. Truth, again, is complex, many-sided, Mill taught. The censor's blade, unlike the surgeon's, should leave room at the margins for partial falsehoods that contain or obscure partial truths. Finally, even if an opinion or idea is totally false, the purveyor of false claims serves an important social function – to revivify our understanding of the truth by forcing those defending it to rethink, and thus to fully re-imagine, our reasons for believing it.

One of the most important areas in which the falsity of a statement is legally significant involves defamation claims. The tort of defamation had traditionally been permitted notwithstanding its restrictive consequences for freedom of speech because slanderous (spoken) or libelous (written or broadcast) opinions concerning another are false and affect the personal reputation of the victim. Thus, traditionally, there were no First Amendment limitations on defamation actions. But in *New York Times* v. *Sullivan*,[69] decided in 1964 – a year before *Griswold* v. *Connecticut* and five years before *Brandenburg* – the Supreme Court applied First Amendment limits to defamation actions.

The *New York Times* carried a full-page ad decrying the response of the police and other city officials in Montgomery, Alabama after a sit-in and other civil rights activities which took place in 1960. The ad claimed that "truckloads of police armed with shotguns and teargas" surrounded the campus at Alabama State and that they padlocked the cafeteria to "starve [students] into submission." It also contained allegations concerning the treatment by local authorities of Dr. Martin Luther King, Jr. Ultimately, the ad contained several misstatements of fact but nowhere mentioned the plaintiff, Sullivan, a city commissioner who claimed the ad had indirectly defamed him.

The Alabama Supreme Court upheld a $500,000 civil judgment against the *New York Times* and various civil rights leaders for the defamation of Sullivan. But the Supreme Court reversed ruling that, in cases involving claims of defamation by public officials, the Constitution created some "breathing space" for false statements. More specifically, the Court held that before a public official could recover for defamation for a claim involving public conduct, the official had to

[69] 376 US 254 (1964).

prove "actual malice" (i.e., that the false and defamatory statements were made "intentionally or with reckless disregard of the truth"). In other words, if a false statement involving public officials was uttered with no more than negligence, it would be constitutionally shielded from a defamation action.

In his opinion for the Court, Justice Brennan cited Mill, declaring that "erroneous statement is inevitable in free debate, and that it must be protected if the freedom of expression are to have the 'breathing space' that they need."[70] This necessary breathing space required that the threat of civil sanctions should not deter speech on a matter of public importance. A few pages later, Brenan quoted Mill directly on the same topic: "Even a false statement may be deemed to make a valuable contribution to public debate, since it brings about [quoting Mill] "the clearer perception and livelier impression of truth, produced by its collision with error."[71] In sum, even false statements can serve the function of vivifying discussion and debate.

The *Sullivan* case has had a powerful effect on defamation claims involving public officials, celebrities and other well-known individuals. The "actual malice" standard has been developed in a series of other cases after the *Sullivan* case. Perhaps the most famous of these was *Hustler Magazine* v. *Falwell*,[72] where the standard was used to immunize *Hustler Magazine*'s parody depicting Reverend Falwell in an incestuous tryst with his mother in a Lynchburg, Virginia, outhouse. The Court here ruled that the "actual malice" standard prevented Falwell not only from recovering for defamation, but for the tort of intentional infliction of emotional distress, a tort that does not necessarily require the making of false statements.

The Supreme Court recently extended constitutional protection for false statements beyond the realm of defamation. In *United States* v. *Alvarez*,[73] it struck down the federal Stolen Valor Act, which made it a federal crime for anyone to falsely state that they had been awarded a decoration or medal for US military service. Alvarez falsely claimed at a public meeting that he had been awarded the Congressional Medal of Honor – a statement made, the Court pointed out, "not to gain a benefit, but in a pathetic attempt to gain respect that eluded him."

Justice Kennedy who, as we will see in the next chapter, is another among the justices who have been deeply influenced by Mill, wrote the majority opinion. Permitting the government to criminalize this, Kennedy worried, would permit the government to "compile a list of subjects about which false statements are

70 *New York Times* v. *Sullivan*, 376 US 254, 272, n. 13 (1964), citing Mill's *On Liberty*.
71 Ibid., at 279, n. 19 (1964).
72 485 US 46 (1988).
73 567 US 709 (2012).

punishable." He then underscored the beneficial consequences of certain kinds of false statements:

> False factual statements can serve useful human objectives, for example: in social contexts, where they may prevent embarrassment, protect privacy, shield a person from prejudice, provide the sick with comfort or preserve a child's innocence; in public contexts, where they may stop a panic or otherwise preserve calm in the face of danger and even in technical, philosophical and scientific contexts where, (as Socrates methods suggest) examination of a false statement (even if made deliberately to mislead) can promote a form of thought that ultimately helps realize the truth ...

Kennedy followed his passage by quoting the same excerpt Justice Brennan had pointed to in *New York Times* v. *Sullivan*.[74]

Freedom of expression is obviously essential to a well-functioning democracy. But Mill was among the first to point out that it may be essential to a healthy society – and, indeed, to the development of well-formed individuals who comprise a healthy society.

[74] "Even a false statement may be deemed to make a valuable contribution to public debate, since it brings about the clearer perception and livelier impression of truth, produced by its collision with error." 567 US at 733.

7

A New Equality

John Stuart Mill is remembered today primarily for his views on freedom both in its negative form (privacy) and in its affirmative form (self-expression). But there is a third important aspect of his thought for which he is, unjustly, seldom remembered at all. Mill was a true egalitarian – and in the modern sense of that word "equality." It was Mill who began to harmonize liberty and equality in a way that led to the modern progressive synthesis of the two values. It was Mill, moreover, who was an impassioned critic of slavery, racism and gender discrimination – at a time when these views were neither popular (even among the intelligentsia) nor considered part of the panoply of "liberal" positions. It was Mill who began to make equality an integral part of liberalism rather than a value in tension with liberty, as classical liberals had seen it.

CONTRASTING VIEWS OF EQUALITY IN CLASSICAL AND PROGRESSIVE LIBERALISM

That liberty and equality conflict is a virtual staple of classical liberal thought. Classical liberals from Locke forward valued *formal* equality, a condition of general equality before the law. As Locke observed in the *Second Treatise*, "all Men by Nature are equal, [but] I cannot be supposed to understand all sorts of Equality... [but only] the equal right that every man hath to his natural Freedom, without being subjected to the will or authority of any other Man."[1]

Later thinkers in this tradition never tired of warning of the counterproductive nature of efforts to legislate equality. "Render possessions ever so equal," David Hume observed, "men's different degrees of art, care and industry will immediately break that equality.

[1] John Locke, *Second Treatise on Government*, sec. 54. Of course, later liberals reinterpreted what it means to be under the will of another so that government might have a role in regulating businesses, family relations and other forms of private power, but the classical liberal notion was clearly limited to enforced servitude, coercion and constraint.

Or if you check these virtues, you reduce society to the most extreme indigence, and instead of preventing want and beggary in a few, render it unavoidable to the whole community."[2] Similarly, James Madison, who was probably influenced by Hume's political thought,[3] made the same point in *Federalist* 10: One way to abolish factions – groups with different economic, political or religious interests – is "by destroying the liberty which is essential to its existence." This would create a kind of equality but:

> the diversity in the faculties of men, from which the rights or property originate, is not less an insuperable obstacle to a uniformity of interests. The protection of these faculties is the first object of government. From the protection of different and unequal faculties of acquiring property, the possession of different degrees and kinds of property immediately results, and from the influence of these on the sentiments and views of different proprietors, ensues a division of the society into different interests and parties.[4]

Only by destroying liberty can a factionless equality be created. Or as F. A. Hayek put it more recently, "equality before the law, which freedom requires, leads to material inequality" so that "the desire of making people more alike in their condition cannot be accepted in a free society."[5]

Progressive liberals of the late nineteenth and twentieth centuries, in contrast, view freedom and equality as coextensive values; they insist that a strong measure of substantive equality is a necessary condition of true freedom. "Liberty without equality," declared L. T. Hobhouse in his concise but masterful account of the intellectual history of liberalism, "is a name of noble sound and squalid result."[6] John Dewey argued during the time of F.D.R.'s "New Deal" that inequality was always a function of class-based denials of freedom:

> The direct impact of liberty always has to do with some class or group that is suffering in a special way from some form of constraint exercised by the distribution of powers that exist in contemporary society. Should a classless society ever come into existence, the formal *concept* of liberty would lose its significance because the fact for which it stands would have become an integral part of the established relations of human beings to one another.[7]

Or as Ronald Dworkin put it more recently, "What does it mean for government to treat its citizens as equals? That is, I think, the same question as what it means for government to treat its citizens as free." If this should leave some uncertainty about

[2] David Hume, *An Enquiry Concerning the Principles of Morals* (Ann Arbor: University of Michigan Library, 1751), part 3, sec. 2.

[3] Douglas Adair, "That Politics May Be Reduced to a Science: Hume, James Madison and the Tenth Federalist" *Fame and the Founding Fathers* (Indianapolis: Liberty Fund, 1974), 132–51.

[4] James Madison, "Federalist 10," in *The Federalist*, ed. Benjamin Fletcher Wright (Cambridge: Harvard University Press, 1961), 130–31.

[5] F. A. Hayek, *The Constitution of Liberty* (Chicago: University of Chicago Press, 1960), 87.

[6] L. T. Hobhouse, *Liberalism* (London: Oxford University Press, 1911), 73.

[7] John Dewey, *Liberty and Social Action* (New York: G. P. Putnam, 1935), 48 (emphasis in original).

what we mean by treating citizens as "free" and "equal", Dworkin continues, "It is obviously obnoxious to the liberal conception [of government] that someone should have more of what the community as a whole has to distribute because he or his father had superior skill or luck."[8] It is striking how different Dworkin's view is from Madison's for whom the protection of "the diversity in the faculties of men," which is the first object of government, would always entail inequality.

What separates Locke, Hume, Madison and Hayek from Hobhouse, Dewey, Dworkin and others is not simply their contrasting ideas of equality. It is also their differing views of freedom. Before equality could take its place among the triumvirate of liberal values, both values had to be rethought. Mill achieved this and, in doing so, ultimately influenced not only our political but our constitutional tradition.

MILL'S EGALITARIAN LIBERTARIANISM

Mill called himself an "advanced Liberal" and an "ideal socialist" and, in various places, made some fairly radical pronouncements about the nature of equality that distance him inexorably from his classical liberal forebears. In his *Autobiography* he endorsed the principle that permitted "no authority in Society whatever over the individual *other than to enforce equal freedom of development over all individualities*."[9] Yet what might this mean? A government with the power to enforce "equal freedom of development" is a government that could potentially redistribute income, impose progressive taxation policies, establish various educational and professional requirements for those born in differing conditions and perhaps even impose limits on speech that might inhibit the free development of those from disadvantaged groups. All of these policies would obviously conflict with Mill's positions on these issues. How could socialism be squared with Mill's fairly libertarian view of government? And how could "equal freedom of development" be achieved with limited government?

Mill sometimes suggested that society, in a collective sense, has the power to compel all individuals to share equally in the labor necessary to maintain the standard of living. In his reply to Thomas Carlyle on "the negro question," for example, he observed that:

> [E]ach person is bound, in justice, to perform his share [of work] and society has an incontestable right to declare to everyone, that if he work not, at this work of necessity, neither shall he eat. Society has not enforced this right, having in so far postponed the rule of justice to other considerations.[10]

[8] Ronald Dworkin, "Liberalism," *A Matter of Principle* (Cambridge: Harvard University Press, 1985), 195.
[9] Mill, *Autobiography*, CW, 1:260.
[10] Mill, "The Negro Question," CW, XXI, 91.

These sentiments anticipate the kind of society George Bernard Shaw and later Fabian socialists sought to establish, in which citizen committees would review, at periodic intervals, the contributions of each citizen. How could Mill – particular the Mill of *On Liberty* – have countenanced such an idea? And if society has "postponed the rule of justice," by what measure might they enforce this once it decides to do so?

Three things must be borne in mind here about how Mill might have thought liberty and a more *substantive* equality could be reconciled.

First, recall that his more "positive" conception of liberty, rooted in the idea of self-individuation, is compatible with the deeper equality of progressives. Theoretically, at least, there was less of a conflict for Mill between liberty and equality because of his conception of liberty. Whereas classical liberals tended to view all laws and regulations as an infringement of freedom (since freedom was virtually defined by the absences of law), Mill could take the view that law can actually advance the cause of freedom by expanding an equal condition of self-development for all. Equality was not *the same thing as freedom*, as it seems to have been for Dworkin, but it was a *necessary condition* for freedom in order for personal autonomy to develop.

Second, Mill's views about the informal uses of social power, the tyranny of the majority and the way customs and tradition inhibit self-individuation open the door to the use of government to advance liberty. If social and economic institutions from corporations to social groups to the family can infringe the "equal freedom of development" which is a part of freedom, might not government limit the limiters? Even in that most libertarian work, *On Liberty*, Mill extended the "harm principle," well beyond government: no group of individuals may coerce an individual who is not harming a third party. If government can stop inappropriate uses of social power which limit individual freedom, why can it not also create conditions of equality? Mill was usually reluctant to take this step but his principle undoubtedly opens the door for later liberals to justify laws, which expand individual freedom by limiting social power and economic power – for example, laws that prohibit business or social groups from excluding women.

Third, Mill was considerably more skeptical than Madison about the causes of inequality. Whereas Madison attributes inequality to the "diversity in the faculties of men," Mill was sure that inequality was the result of circumstance, social conditions and the influence of environment. He discussed this topic, which he called "ethnology," in his first work, *A System of Logic*.[11] When inequality is the result of innate differences between two individuals, the case for intervention to create equality is less compelling. But when inequality is a function of social factors, doesn't government have a powerful reason to intervene, that is, to use law to counteract socially produced inequalities?

[11] He first began to explore "ethnology," in his *System of Logic*. J. S. Mill, *A System of Logic*, CW, 8:861–74. He developed these ideas years later in his *Subjection of Women*.

In each of these ways, Mill's conception of liberty can be harmonized with his conception of equality. The more vexing question, however, is how these two values can be achieved without expanding government. Certainly Mill's *principles* open the door to more government, but in his own *application* of these principles, he usually steered a more libertarian course. He remained genuinely skeptical of expanding government – even when doing so might be thought, in the short term at least, to enlarge liberty and equality. Indeed, in his discussion of the "applications" of his theory in Chapter V of *On Liberty*, he wrote that this was "one of the most difficult and complicated questions in the art of government."[12] He worried in a letter he had written to Harriet around the time he conceived the idea for *On Liberty* that "most of the projects of social reformers are usually liberticide."[13] And he remained skeptical about the expansion of government power, especially when a public "accustomed to expect everything be done for them by the State… naturally hold the State responsible for all evil which befalls them."[14]

How, in sum, could Mill hope to advance his version of liberalism while retaining the essentially libertarian view of government? We can ask two questions here: Was Mill aware of this conflict between his libertarianism and his egalitarian principles? And was he too optimistic about the prospects of reconciling true egalitarianism with limited government power? The answers to these questions are – yes, and yes.

Mill was certainly aware of the tension but he could afford to believe that liberty and equality might grow together, without massive government, for two reasons. First, he lived at a time when many of the positions of advanced liberals like himself depended more on the *elimination* of bad (i.e., freedom-limiting) laws rather than on the expansion of good (i.e., freedom-promoting) laws. A good libertarian could then still look like a committed egalitarian. Slavery had been imposed through law, after all, as had other forms of racial discrimination including the discrimination later inflicted during the Jim Crow era. Remove these laws and the cause of equality would be improved. Similarly, all of the legal disabilities of women (i.e., those which prohibited them from voting or which delegated the ownership of women's property to their husbands) were achieved through laws which, Mill argued, should be repealed. In each of these cases – by eliminating oppressive laws – the cause of equality would advance hand-in-hand with the cause of liberty.

Second, Mill thought that the most important social mechanism for achieving the concurrent advance of equality and liberty, while simultaneously abstaining from expanding government, was through the diversity of social institutions. Even in the provision of the most important social services, the state should at most serve only a supporting role in promoting the necessary social diversity. Thus, even in the context of education, which Mill valued above almost all other practices and

12 Mill, *On Liberty*, *CW*, 18:308–9.

13 Mill to Harriet (January 15, 1855), *CW*, 14:294.

14 Mill, *On Liberty*, *CW*, 18:307.

institutions, the state's role should be limited: "An education established and controlled by the State," he wrote in *On Liberty*, "should only exist, *if it exists at all*, as one among many competing experiments, carried on for the purpose of example and stimulus, to keep the others up to a certain standard of excellence."[15]

Thus, Mill hoped that equality could be achieved, in large measure, by the decentralization of power and the diversification of social institutions. It is a noble vision but it is here that Mill was too optimistic – both about the prospects for limiting the expansion of state power and about the chances of achieving the necessary social diversity without it.

MILL ON RACE AND GENDER

Mill's most important writings on racial and gender equality are assembled in volume XXI of his *Collected Works*. His three most important essays on race are "The Negro Question" (1850), "The Contest in America" (1862) and "The Slave Power" (1862). The first two were published in *Fraser's Review* and the last in the *Westminster Review*. His most important book on the equality of the sexes was *The Subjection of Women* (1869), but he also wrote several important essays on marriage, spousal assault and other topics.

"The Negro Question" was Mill's response to Thomas Carlyle's "Occasional Discourse on the Negro Question," an essay which suggested that the Jamaican population, which had been emancipated from slavery in 1834, had been better off under the yoke. Anticipating the argument he later made in *The Subjection of Women*, Mill observed, in true progressive fashion, that human history consists of a gradual, if hard-won, overcoming of tyranny and social injustice.[16] What was true in the context of gender was equally valid in that of race. In "The Negro Question," he declared that the "history of human improvement is the record of a struggle by which inch after inch of ground has been wrang from these maleficent powers, and more and more of human life rescued from the iniquitous domain of the law of might."[17] Here Mill condemned slavery and the "owners of human flesh" in the fiercest of terms:

> For nearly two centuries had negroes, and many thousands annually, been seized by force or treachery and carried off to the West Indies to be worked to death, literally to death, for it was the received maxim, the acknowledged dictate of good economy, to wear them out quickly and import more.[18]

Central to his attack on inequality was his critique of one of its most important pillars: the claim that inequality is usually a function of "innate differences" between

[15] Ibid., 302 (emphasis mine).

[16] As Mill later wrote in *The Subjection of Women*, "the tendencies of progressive human society afford not only no presumption in favor of this system of inequality of rights, but a strong one against it." Mill, *The Subjection of Women*, CW, 21:272.

[17] Mill, "The Negro Question," CW, 21:87.

[18] Ibid., 88.

the races. If Carlyle had bothered to consider the true causes of human behavior – causes which were social and economic in nature – "he would have escaped the vulgar error of imputing every difference which he finds in human beings to an original difference in nature. ... Is nothing to be attributed to soil, nothing to climate, nothing to difference of exposure?"[19] But if there are no "innate differences" between the races, why had European civilization advanced, as Carlyle declared, so far beyond that of African culture? Mill answered: "If the trees grew near together, may not the one which, by whatever accident, grew up first, have retarded the other's development by its shade?" Indeed, he went further. He was the first, as far as I know, to make the claim that Greek civilization, which had been recognized for 2500 years as the foundation of western civilization ever since, had borrowed it most important ideas from the Egyptians – and that the Egyptians were, "a negro civilization."[20] Mill's essay ends by condemning Carlyle's piece as "a true work of the devil."[21]

"The Contest in America" and "The Slave Power" were both written near the onset of the Civil War. In the first of these, Mill characteristically attacked the then-popular position in England, which favored the South. He criticized the rationalization that the War was really about secession, not slavery, he predicted that the North could win "if their present determination holds... for they are twice as numerous, and ten or twelve times and rich,"[22] and he brought to bear a moral barrage which isolated the South as the sole standout in the World on the issue of slavery: "When men set themselves up, in defiance of the rest of the world, to do the devil's work, no good can come of them until the world has made them feel that the work cannot suffer to be done any longer."[23]

"The Slave Power" was an extended endorsement of J. E. Cairnes' book of the same name. But it was also an analysis of the economic and cultural effects of slavery, which leaves only three classes in the South – "the slaves, on whom devolves all the regular industry; the slaveholders, who reap all its fruits, and an idle and lawless rabble [the 'mean whites' or 'white trash,' as he calls them earlier] who live dispersed over vast plains in a condition little removed from absolute barbarism."[24]

Mill was a fierce opponent of racism, but he had far more to say about inequality in the context of gender. Though he is seldom remembered for it today, he was among the "first wave" of feminist thinkers in the nineteenth century – long before feminism was intellectually fashionable even among self-described "liberals." Mill did not parrot the feminist positions of others: he *developed* them and he *integrated* them into the foundation of liberal individualism. For, again, the point was not about equality: it was about autonomy for all. Equality was but a necessary condition for autonomy.

19 Ibid., 93.
20 Ibid., 93.
21 Ibid., 95.
22 Mill, "The Contest in America," CW, 21:138.
23 Ibid., 139.
24 Mill, "The Slave Power," CW, 21:150.

The last work of Mill's to be published during his lifetime was *The Subjection of Women*, a thorough-going legal, political and sociological critique of existing social institutions in regard to gender differences. He had originally written the book in 1861 but held off from publishing it until 1869, suspecting that it would be his least well-received book. In some ways, he was correct. Even such close associates as Alexander Bain dismissed Mill's "doctrine of natural equality" as the single greatest mistake of an otherwise great "scientific thinker."[25] Yet Mill was wrong about the unpopularity of the book: the first two editions sold out within a few months.[26]

In *Subjection*, Mill vigorously argued that women should be politically and legally equal to men in every way – that they should have the right to vote,[27] to hold office[28] and to possess the same property rights as men.[29] He strenuously opposed the age-old tradition of making the husband the owner of the wife's property upon marriage.[30] (While in Parliament, he supported the Married Women's Property Bill, which ultimately ended this practice.[31]) He argued for full equality in the professions, expecting that, if there were natural differences between men and women, they would play themselves out in the competition for jobs. "What women by nature cannot do," he wrote in *Subjection of Women*, "it is quite superfluous to forbid them from doing."[32] He made strategic concessions to the *status quo*, but never abandoned his principles. Thus, while he thought that, in a wage-earning society, the best arrangement was generally for the man to earn the family's living while the wife attended the home and children,[33] he went on to caution that every woman has the right to choose for herself whether to work or stay at home and that "the utmost latitude ought to exist for the adaptation of general rules to individual suitabilities."[34]

[25] Alexander Bain, *John Stuart Mill: A Criticism with Personal Recollections* (New York: Longmans, Green and Company, 1882), 146.

[26] Stefan Collini, Introduction, *CW*, 21:xiii.

[27] "To have a vote in choosing those by whom one is to be governed is a means of self-protection due to every one. … Under whatever condition, and within whatever limits, men are admitted to the suffrage; there is not a shadow of justification for not admitting women under the same." Mill, *Subjection of Women*, *CW*, 21:301.

[28] Ibid.

[29] Ibid., at 296–97.

[30] Ibid.

[31] Mill, "Public and Parliamentary Speeches," *CW*, 28:283–86 (June 10, 1868). The bill passed in 1870, after Mill had been voted out of office.

[32] Mill, *Subjection of Women*, *CW*, 21:280, Not anticipating the argument that would made later by proponents of affirmative action for women that prejudice, rather than natural ability, would keep them from certain jobs, he continued on, "What they can do, but not as well as the men who are their competitors, competition suffices to exclude them from, since nobody asks for protective duties and bounties in favor of women." Ibid.

[33] "When the support of the family depends not on property, but on earnings, the common arrangement by which the man earns the income and the wife superintends the domestic expenditure, seems to me the most suitable division of labor between the two persons." Ibid., *supra* note 76, at 297. Mill went on to observe that, when women work, men seldom perform their end of the bargain with house and children. Ibid.

[34] Ibid., at 298.

Mill's political and social conclusions were all linked to his deeper sociological observation that it is almost impossible to separate the effects of biology from the effects of social institutions. In his *System of Logic*, which laid the groundwork for all of his subsequent work in political and economic issues, he had argued that most or all of the supposed differences between men and women are likely to be the product of social, rather than biological, factors. "A long list of mental and moral differences are observed, or supposed, to exist between men and women: but at some future and, it may be hoped, not distant period, equal freedom and an equally independent social position, come to be possessed by both, and their differences of character are either removed or totally altered."[35]

He amplified this in the *Subjection of Women*. So little was understood about the sociological effects of cultural norms on gender that no one had the right to justify inequalities on the basis of "natural differences" between the sexes:

> The profoundest knowledge of the laws of the formation of character is indispensable to entitle anyone to affirm even that there is any difference, much more what the difference is, between the two sexes considered as moral and rational beings; and since no one, as yet, has that knowledge (for there is hardly any subject which, in proportion to its importance, has been so little studied), no one is thus far entitled to any positive opinion on the subject.[36]

Women are victims of their dependence on men – a culturally imposed dependence.[37] It is not biology but our social institutions that enable "men [to think] it a clever thing to insult women for being what men made them."[38]

The single greatest barrier to true equality for women, Mill argued, was their socially assigned sexual and procreative function. As he wrote emphatically in a diary entry, if we want to improve human life, we have to de-emphasize sex. But de-emphasizing sex requires that "women should cease to be set apart for this [procreative] function, and should be admitted to all other duties and occupations on a par with men."[39]

This view of sex and procreation dovetailed with Mill's (and Harriet's) libertarian views on marriage and divorce. Freeing women from the procreative function

[35] Mill, *System of Logic*, CW, 8:868.

[36] Mill, *Subjection of Women*, CW, 21:277–78.

[37] Sex and child-rearing were, in turn, linked to the dependence of women on their husbands. Mill had read his Rousseau who had written that "it is impossible to make any man a slave unless he is first reduced to a situation in which he cannot do without the help of others" Jean-Jacques Rousseau, Discourse on the Origin of Inequality, in *The Social Contract and the Discourses* (New York: Alfred H. Knopf, 1973), 81. As Mill put it in a letter to Harriet, "The first and indispensable step, therefore, toward the enfranchisement of woman, is that she be educated, so as not to be dependent either on her father or husband for subsistence … women will never be what they should be … until women, as universally as men, have the power of gaining their own livelihood." Cited in Nicholas Capalid, *John Stuart Mill: A Biography* (Cambridge: Cambridge University Press, 2004), 106.

[38] Mill, *Subjection of Women*, CW, 21:292.

[39] Mill, "Diary of (8 Jan. – 15 Apr., 1854)," CW, 27:664 (Entry of March 26, 1854).

required giving them (and, of course, their husbands) the legal latitude to divorce at will. In *On Liberty*, Mill approved of von Humboldt's assertion that ending a marriage "should require nothing more than the declared will of either party to dissolve it."[40] While the marital commitment creates a *moral* obligation to the other person and to any children born of the relationship, this obligation need not be fulfilled "at all costs to the happiness of the reluctant party."[41] The unhappy spouse should consider the effects of divorce on their partner and children, but this purely moral obligation "ought to make no difference in the *legal* freedom of the parties to release themselves from the engagement."[42] In sum, there should be an absolute right to divorce and no social compulsion to marry in the first place.

Of course, Mill's and Harriet's views on this developed in the context of their own experiences during the twenty-year period when Harriet remained married to John Taylor. But their "liberal" views on the family were not far removed from the views of such radical thinkers as Marx, Engels and Emma Goldman, among others. The traditional household, Mill wrote in the *Subjection of Women*, was a "school of despotism" when is should be a "school of sympathy and equality, of living together in love, without power on one side and obedience on the other."[43] He tied these views to his general understanding of society as an evolving set of institutions which has moved through an initial stage of paternal despotism, a second stage, influenced by Christian morals, where the husband's power is tempered by beneficence, to a third stage where social relations should be based on simple equality: "We have had the morality of submission, and the morality of chivalry and generosity; the time is now come for the morality of justice."[44]

These sentiments expressed throughout Mill's career – from the early *System of Logic* (1843) to *On Liberty* (1859) to the *Subjection of Women* (1869) – make clear not only that Mill was a committed feminist from beginning to end but that, more generally, he viewed liberty and equality not as contrary, but as co-sympathetic values. Both were aspects, ultimately, of his more general, if subliminal, conception of social justice.

THE SUPREME COURT'S EQUAL PROTECTION JURISPRUDENCE

The Equal Protection clause was one of the three rights-bearing clauses of the Fourteenth Amendment, ratified in 1868, along with the Privileges or Immunities and the Due Process clauses. Whereas the Privileges or Immunities clause was interpreted out of the Constitution in the *Slaughterhouse Cases* of 1873, the Due

[40] Mill, *On Liberty*, *CW*, 18:300.

[41] Ibid.

[42] Ibid., 301. In sum, there is an absolute legal right to divorce even if the divorcing party "is morally responsible for the wrong." Ibid.

[43] Mill, *Subjection of Women*, *CW*, 21:295.

[44] Ibid., at 294.

Process clause soon gained traction as the vehicle for "freedom of contract" during the Lochner era. Thus, the former clause was eliminated by judicial construction while the latter was reinterpreted to do the work of the former.

The *Slaughterhouse* Court interpreted the Equal Protection clause, on the other hand, as being limited to racial, as opposed to other forms of discrimination – which was precisely its original purpose. The Court rejected the claims of butchers who had argued that a corporate charter requiring butchers to work at an assigned place treated them differently from other occupations in violation of the Equal Protection clause.

Even when the Court used the clause to strike down racially discriminatory laws, it did so initially in a limited way. In 1880, in *Strauder* v. *West Virginia*, for example, the Court held unconstitutional a state law prohibiting African-Americans from sitting on juries.[45] Here the law plainly discriminated on the face of the statute and the Court held it unconstitutional. It went a little further in 1886, holding in *Yick Wo* v. *Hopkins*, that "facially neutral" laws – laws which do not discriminate on the face of the statute but which are applied in a racially discriminatory way – are also unconstitutional.[46] In this case, a San Francisco ordinance required approval before a laundry could be operated in a wooden building. On its face, the statue applied to everyone equally. But the City granted licenses to only one in two hundred Chinese applicants, while granting almost all applications from white applicants.

But this was as far as the Court was willing to go at this point. In *Pace* v. *Alabama*, decided in 1883, a black man and a white woman were convicted and sentenced to two years in prison for living together. The Court rejected an Equal Protection challenge to the convictions because, in its view, there was no discrimination: since both had been sentenced to the same prison term, there was no denial of "equal protection of the law." Similarly, in *Plesy* v. *Ferguson*, a case decided a decade after *Yick Wo*, the Court refused to extend equal protection coverage to so-called "separate but equal" conditions.[47] Since whites could not sit in a car reserved for blacks, blacks were not discriminated against by being prohibited from sitting with whites. It took more than a half-century to overrule these cases in *Loving* v. *Virginia*[48] and *Brown* v. *Board of Education*[49] and, in doing so, adopt the principle that Equal Protection forbids lawmakers from taking race into account in any way.

[45] 100 US 303 (1880).

[46] 118 US 356 (1986). The San Francisco ordinance required approval before a laundry could be operated in a wooden building. Thus, the statute itself was not racially discriminatory. But the City granted licenses to only one in 200 Chinese applicants, while granting almost all applications from white applicants.

[47] *Plesy* v. *Ferguson*, 163 US 537 (1896) (upholding from constitutional attack a law requiring blacks and whites to sit in separate compartments in railroad cars).

[48] *Loving* v. *Virginia*, 388 US 1 (1967).

[49] *Brown* v. *Board of Education*, 347 US 483 (1954).

In the period immediately following the adoption of the Fourteenth Amendment, few seem to have imagined that Equal Protection might extend to other categories such as gender. In fact, just a day after the *Slaughterhouse* cases were decided, the Court held that the Fourteenth Amendment did not guarantee women the right to hold a license to practice law.[50] What makes this case particularly striking is that it never even mentions the Equal Protection clause. The Court seems not to have even contemplated that Equal Protection principles might extend to gender discrimination. Instead, it held that the petitioner, Myra Bradwell, had no "privilege" to practice law under the Privileges or Immunities clause. In his concurring opinion, Justice Bradley intuits – and rejects – Mill's claim that the greatest obstacle to equality between men and women is a woman's preordained role in the family. Remarkably, he wrote that while a law prohibiting women from the practice of law "undoubtedly deprives her of liberty and property interests" under the Due Process clause, "the harmony, not to say identity, of interests which belong or should belong to the family institution, is repugnant to the idea of a woman adopting a distinct and independent career from that of her husband."[51]

This trend continued apace for roughly a century. In *Minor* v. *Happersett*, decided two years after *Bradwell*, in 1875, the Court refused to extend equal protection coverage to a woman's right to vote.[52] In *Muller* v. *Oregon*, it refused to extend *Lochner's* protection of freedom of contract to women, upholding a law prohibiting women from working more than ten hours per day in factories.[53] So limited was the perceived scope of the Equal Protection clause well into the twentieth century that in 1927, in an opinion upholding the compelled sterilization of a woman, Justice Oliver Wendell Holmes dismissed her Equal Protection claim as "the usual last resort of constitutional arguments."[54]

Yet all of this began to change with *Brown* v. *Board of Education*. Indeed, most legal scholars view Brown as much more than the first modern Equal Protection case. They see it as the case that opened up what we called in Chapter 4 the "modern liberal" era of constitutional rights protection. By the 1960s and 1970s, the Court began to use the Equal Protection clause more widely – not only in ways that had nothing to do with race, but in ways which made it evident that equality and freedom were intimately linked in the modern constitutional vision. In *Harper* v. *Virginia Board of Electors*, it used the Equal Protection clause to strike down a state poll tax which charged a $1.50 fee to vote. Justice Douglas's opinion argued that the tax discriminated against the poor, since the burden of the tax fell more heavily on the poor.

[50] 83 US 130 (1873).
[51] 83 US at 133.
[52] 88 US 162 (1875).
[53] 208 US 412 (1908).
[54] *Buck* v. *Bell*, 274 US 200, 208 (1927). See Stephen A. Siegel, "Justice Holmes, *Buck* v. *Bell* and the History of Equal Protection," 90 *Minnesota Law Review* 106 (2005).

But he linked the Equal Protection analysis to the First Amendment freedom of expression which was linked, in turn, to the right to vote.[55] The constitutional force of the opinion, in other words, depends on the intersection of freedom and equality.

In *Shapiro* v. *Thompson*, the Court struck down a requirement of California law that applicants for welfare benefits had to live in the state for at least a year.[56] The state had argued that the law was intended to reserve welfare benefits for California residents and prevent non-residents from coming to California simply to take advantage of its higher welfare rates. But the Court, in an opinion written by Justice Brennan, said that the law infringed the values of freedom and equality – that it discriminated against those most likely to apply for welfare benefits (implicating equal protection) by affecting their fundamental right to travel (implicating their liberty interest).

In other cases during this same era, the Court used the Equal Protection clause to strike down laws that drew distinctions on the basis of alienage (i.e., between citizens and non-citizens),[57] laws that discriminated against unmarried persons,[58] statutes that disadvantaged children born out of wedlock,[59] laws that discriminated against custodial fathers who were unmarried to the children's mother,[60] a federal law which allegedly targeted, under food stamp assistance programs, people living in "hippie communes"[61] and a zoning law used to disadvantage the mentally disabled.[62] All but the last of these cases were decided in a seven-year period, from 1966 (the year after the Griswold privacy decision) to 1973 (the year *Roe* v. *Wade* was decided).

55 *Harper* v. *Virginia Board of Elections*, 383 US 663 (1966), was decided just a year after *Griswold* v. *Connecticut*.

56 394 US 618 (1969).

57 *In Sugarman* v. *Dugall*, 413 US 634 (1973), the Court held unconstitutional a New York law which prohibited resident aliens (non-citizens who held a green card) from holding state civil service jobs. The Court used strict scrutiny, using the same high standard it uses for racial discrimination.

58 *Eisenstadt* v. *Baird*, 406 US 430 (1972), used the Equal Protection clause to extend the right to privacy to unmarried people. The case was, in one sense, about freedom – the right to contraception – but the Court achieved this result by holding that there was no rational basis for distinguishing married from unmarried persons in this context.

59 *Weber* v. *Aetna Casualty and Surety Co.*, 406 US 164 (1972) held unconstitutional a law that excluded non-marital children from workers compensation statutes.

60 In *Stanley* v. *Illinois*, 405 US 645 (1972), the Court held unconstitutional a law that required the removal of children from the custody of a father when the father had not been married to children's mother. In this case, the couple had lived together up until the death of the mother.

61 In *US Department of Agriculture* v. *Moreno*, 413 US 528 (1973), the Court struck down a provision of the federal food stamp law that prohibited unrelated person living together in the same house or apartment from receiving food stamps. The law may have been motivated by animus against "hippie communes" who were using food stamps. The Court used the Equal Protection clause holding that the purpose of the law was illegitimate because it was a form of political animus against an unpopular group. The Court's concern with protecting unpopular groups is consistent with Mill's insistence that a free society permits "experiments in lifestyle."

62 *City of Cleburne* v. *Cleburne Living Center*, 473 US 432 (1985). Here the Court struck down a zoning ordinance that was used to prevent the creation of a home for mentally disabled persons. The Court observed that zoning permits were permitted for most other uses including fraternity houses and nursing homes.

That there was such an explosion of activity under the Equal Protection clause during the same heady period in which other constitutional developments inspired by Mill began to take root in the soil of our constitutional tradition suggests a deeper origin and commonality among these decisions. Underlying each of these cases – cases involving rights to contraception, to live in socially alternative circumstances such as a commune, to raise children out of wedlock, etc. – is the idea that autonomous individuality is linked to an "equal freedom of development of all individualities." Even if Mill's influence here was too diffused to credit him directly with these developments – for surely there were many more recent causes – it is no coincidence that these multifarious constitutional developments "broke through" at roughly the same time in our legal tradition. Several of the opinions here had been written by Justices Douglas and Brennan, who, as we have seen in the previous two chapters, knew and frequently quoted Mill.

MILL, MODERN EQUAL PROTECTION AND GENDER

It is in the context of gender, however, that we find striking parallels to several of Mill's arguments and observations made in *The Subjection of Women*. Indeed, we see this in the very first case in which the Court used the Equal Protection clause to hold a law unconstitutional for gender discrimination.

The year was 1971 and the case, *Reed* v. *Reed*, involved a challenge to a state statute requiring a preference for male over female administrators of a relative's estate.[63] This was a case involving a divorcing couple each of whom sought to be named administrator to the estate of their deceased son. An Idaho statute required a preference, in the naming of an administrator, for male over female relatives in each class – sons over daughters, husbands over wives, fathers over mothers. Mrs. Reed, the mother of the deceased, challenged this probate provision but the Idaho Supreme Court held that the objective of the statute was simply "to eliminate one area of controversy when two or more persons, equally entitled seek letters of administration."[64] But the Supreme Court rejected this easy rationale:

> To give a mandatory preference to members of either sex over members of the other, merely to accomplish the elimination of hearings on the merits, is to make the very kind of arbitrary legislative choice forbidden by the Equal Protection Clause of the Fourteenth Amendment; and whatever may be said as to the positive values of avoiding intra-family controversy, the choice in this context may not lawfully be mandated solely on the basis of sex.[65]

[63] 404 US 71 (1971) (holding unconstitutional under the Equal Protection clause an Idaho statute that required sons be preferred to daughters, husbands to wives, brothers to sisters, etc.) in the appointment of administrators of an estate. In this case, a divorcing couple each sought to be named the administrator of their deceased son's estate.

[64] 404 US at 76.

[65] Ibid., at 76–77.

This was precisely the same argument Mill had made in *The Subjection of Women*: "It is quite true that things that have to be decided every day ... ought to depend on one will; one person must have their sole control. But it does not follow that this should always be the same person."[66]

Mill's suspicion that culture and circumstance frequently play a much greater role than biology in matters involving asserted differences between the sexes has been vindicated in several Supreme Court cases. *Craig* v. *Boren* was the first case in which the Court began to use intermediate scrutiny for gender discrimination under the Equal Protection clause.[67] It was also a case in which men were the purported victims of gender discrimination. The Court took issue with a law that permitted young women, but not men, to drink low-alcohol beer: the law was predicated on questionable statistical claims that young men were more likely to over-drink than women – claims that reflected cultural, rather than biological differences between men and women. The Court, for example, noted that the statistical evidence that men were more frequently involved in traffic accidents failed to account for the fact that men drove more frequently than women, and that intoxicated girls were more likely to be escorted home, rather than arrested.[68] Similarly, in *Stanton* v. *Stanton*, it rejected a law based on "old notions" that required parents to support sons until 21, but daughters only until the age of 18.[69]

As we have seen, Mill was particularly skeptical that we could say anything about "innate differences" between men and women given the tendency for social patterns to mask true abilities of women in physical and intellectual tasks:

> The profoundest knowledge of the laws of the formation of character is indispensable to entitle anyone to affirm even that there is any difference, much less what the difference is, between the two sexes ... no one is thus far entitled to any positive opinion on the subject. Conjectures are all that can at present be made; conjectures that are more or less probable...[70]

Legally, the only way to reinforce this protocol of skepticism would be through a presumption against laws that draw distinctions on the basis of these supposed differences. In the most important decision on gender equality, *United States* v. *Virginia*, the Court required exactly this kind of presumption.[71] In this case, the

66 Mill, *Subjection of Women*, *CW*, 21:291.

67 *Craig* v. *Boren*, 429 US 190 (1976), "Intermediate scrutiny" requires that laws which distinguish on the basis of gender must be "substantially related to an important government purpose." This is a more exacting standard than used in other cases not involving race or gender. It is, however, less exacting than the standard used for racial discrimination, which is why it is an "intermediate" level of scrutiny.

68 Ibid., n. 14.

69 The old notion was that women tend to marry earlier than men, and that men need more time to acquire an education to support their family. *Stanton* v. *Stanton*, 421 US 7 (1975).

70 Mill, *Subjection of Women*, *CW*, 21:277–78.

71 *United States* v. *Virginia*, 518 US 515 (1996).

Court overturned the male-only admissions policy of the Virginia Military Institute, rejecting the state's claim that women could not withstand the rigorous "adversative method" used to train and discipline male military recruits.[72] In the opinion, written by Justice Ginsburg, it added a new requirement to the "intermediate scrutiny" test used in gender equality cases: government must show an "exceedingly persuasive justification" before drawing any gender-based legal distinctions.[73]

Mill's views of gender equality are linked, as we have seen, to his views of marriage and the procreative role of women and men. One interesting contrast between Mill and the modern Supreme Court concerns his view of the power of the state in relation to children. Though he held a libertarian view of the right of divorce, his position concerning the protection of the rights of children to parental support was far more conservative than even modern Supreme Court jurisprudence. In a passage where Mill discusses the right of society to enforce public obligations, he indicates that where "a man fails to perform his legal duties to others, as for instance to support his children, it is no tyranny to force him to fulfill that obligation by compulsory labor if no other means are available."[74] Moreover, the state can justifiably require, as a condition for marriage, that the parties be able to demonstrate in advance that they will be able to support their offspring. Thus, Mill insisted that "[t]he laws which, in many countries on the Continent, forbid marriage unless the parties can show that they have the means to support a family do not exceed the legitimate power of the State."[75] In contrast, the Supreme Court held in *Zablocki* v. *Redhail* that it was a violation of the equal protection clause and the right to marry for a state to require that applicants for a marriage license demonstrate that they are current in child support payments for their previously born children.[76] Where the Court has prioritized the right to marry, Mill would have given preference to the claims of the partners' previously existing children in the event that the new marriage compromised the children's interests.[77]

In sum, Mill's positions on marriage and divorce differ modestly from the modern Supreme Court's rulings in the particulars: the Supreme Court has refused to restrict the right to marry in cases where Mill thought the state has an interest in

[72] Ibid., at 523.

[73] "Virginia has shown no exceedingly persuasive justification for excluding all women from the citizen-soldier training afforded by VMI." Ibid., at 529.

[74] Mill, *On Liberty*, *CW*, 18:295.

[75] Ibid., at 304.

[76] 434 US 374 (1978). Perhaps these conclusions indicate that more freedom requires more responsibility, that a regime of augmented rights may, in some cases, require the willingness to use authoritarian modes of enforcement when the individual has abused his freedom.

[77] Of course, the Court's position in *Zablocki* may have been motivated less by abstract concerns with the potentially conflicting liberty interests of parents and children than with the pragmatic recognition that, in today's society, marriage is no longer a culturally required prerequisite to having children. To the extent that Mill's position was motivated by the apprehension that the children of a second union might be preferred to those of the first, or that both might be impoverished, the modern social reality is that the danger would exist today whether or not the partners marry.

limiting it, and the Court has not created a constitutional right to divorce, as Mill might have preferred (though the same result has been largely effected through the legislative process).[78]

CONCLUSION

In the end, we can, of course, question the extent to which Mill *directly* influenced the equal protection jurisprudence of gender in the 1970s and afterward. We might wonder whether these constitutional developments were instead a result of the influence of "second wave" feminist thinkers in the 1960s and '70s, or even of general cultural changes occurring at the time. Certainly, these other factors played a significant role in the Court's approach to gender.

And, yet, three things are undeniable. First, Mill is one of feminism's *original* defenders. Along with Mary Wollstonecraft, William Godwin (Wollstonecraft's husband), and socialist thinker, Charles Fourier, who first coined the term "feminism," Mill must be counted a seminal thinker among feminism's intellectual pantheon and credited for the influence of his ideas on later thinkers. Second, Mill made the case for feminism fully a century before the "second wave" feminists of the 1960s and '70s. The association of the feminist cause with the name of the greatest public intellectual of the nineteenth century lent feminism an intellectual pedigree that it might not have had without him. Finally, Mill's argument for feminism is integral to the broader fabric of his social thought including the sociological observations of *A System of Logic*, where he argued at length that many of the differences between men and women once thought to be "essential" were in fact caused by social, rather than innate biological factors.

In sum, Mill's case for feminism was not sui generis. It did not stand on its own terms but was instead part of a genuinely comprehensive view of human freedom – a view which tied the cause of feminism closely to the cause of liberalism.

[78] Since about 1970, virtually every state has moved to a no-fault divorce law which gives either spouse a right to divorce for any reason whatsoever.

Index

abortion, 92–95
Abrams v. United States, 101, 109
Adams, John, 28, 63
Adkins v. Children's Hospital, 72, 75
Allgeyer v. Louisiana, 70
Aristotle, 28–29, 38, 47, 48, 104
Auguste Comte and Positivism, 24
autonomy, 2, 22, 25, 26, 35, 36, 47, 59, 73, 74, 86, 87, 89, 90, 91, 92, 96, 97, 101, 102, 123, 126

bad tendency test, 108. *See also* freedom of expression
Bain, Alexander, 7, 15, 39, 127
Belle Terra v. Boraas, 94
Bentham, Jeremy, 7
  liberalism of, 31–34
  Mill's criticism of, 40–41
  as secular thinker, 32
Bill of Rights, rights protected by, 61
Bowers v. Hardwick, 96, 97
Bradley, Justice Joseph P., 68, 69, 70, 131
Bradwell v. Illinois, 131
Brandeis, Justice Louis, Mill's influence on, 3, 83–84
Brandenburg v. Ohio, 58, 113
Brennan, Justice William, 90, 91, 118, 119, 132
Brown v. Board of Education, 130, 131
Burger, Chief justice Warren, 115
Byron, Lord, 42

Calder v. Bull, 64. *See also* natural law; natural rights
Cantwell v. Connecticut, 114
Carey v. Population Services, 91
Carlyle, Thomas, 3, 13, 14, 122, 125
  racism of, 126
Chapters on Socialism, 25, 52
Chase, Justice Samuel, 64
children, obligation to support, 135
choice-making as important to freedom, 46–47
Chomsky, Noam, 53
classical liberalism
  Bentham *versus* Locke, 34
  conception of freedom. *See negative liberty*
  equality, view of, 120
  view of moralism, 80–81
classical political thought, 28–29
clear and present danger test, 112
Cohen v. California, 101, 116
Coleridge, Samuel, 12, 42
Comte, Auguste, 12, 24
Condorcet, Marquis de, 35
Considerations on Representative Government, 23, 84
constitutional history
  republican era of, 60–63
  three periods of, 58–59
Contracts clause, 63
Cooley, Thomas, 69, 84
Coppage v. Kansas, 72
Craig v. Boren, 134

Debs, Eugene, 109
Declaration of Independence, 68
defamation, 117. *See also* freedom of expression
Dennis v. United States, 112
Descartes, Rene, 42, 44
Dewey, John, 121
Divorce right in Mill's view, 129

Douglas, Justice William O., 2, 74, 86, 88, 89, 90, 91, 93, 112–13, 114, 131
 compares Mill and Jefferson, 112
 freedom of expression, defense of, 113
 Mill's influence on, 3
 plagiarizes Mill, 93–94
Dred Scott, 1
Due Process clause, 57, 61, 64, 65, 66, 67, 69, 70, 72, 73, 75, 76, 77, 86, 87, 88, 90, 92, 95, 99, 129–30, 131
Dworkin, Ronald, 121

economic liberties. *See freedom of contract*
Eisenstadt v. Baird, 90, 132
empiricism, 43. *See also* positivism, meaning of
equal freedom of development, 2, 52, 122, 123, 133
equal protection
 and alienage, 132
 and gender, 133–36
 and race, 129–33
Equal Protection clause, 66, 67, 86, 87, 90, 94, 95, 97, 129, 131, 132, 133, 134
 early treatment of, 130
equality
 contrasting views of, 122
 versus freedom, 123–25
 Mill's view of, 122–24
 modern liberal view of, 121–22
ethology, 44
Examination of Sir William Hamilton's Philosophy, An, 23, 44

family autonomy, constitutional right of, 73–74
FCC v. Pacifica Foundation, 116
federalism, 58, 60
Federalist 10, 60, 121
Federalist 78, 63
Federalists and Anti-federalists, 27–28
feminism
 and liberalism, 136
 Mill's, 3–4, 129–36
Fichte, Johann Gottlieb, 12, 35, 37, 42
Field, Justice Stephen J., 68
Fourier, Charles, 22, 136
Frankfurter, Justice Felix, 88
freedom, internal *versus* external senses of, 35
freedom of contract, 71–72. *See also Lochner v. New York*
freedom of expression
 bad tendency test, 108
 defamation and false statements of fact, 119
 development of Holmes's and Brandeis's views on, 108–12
 Mill's contribution to, 101–6
 pornography and offensive speech, 113–16
 three justifications for, 100–1
Friedman, Milton, 53

gay rights, 97–98
gender equality
 Mill's defense of, 129–36
 and the right to serve in the military, 134–35
German idealism, 42
Gitlow v. New York, 110
gnosticism, 42
Goldberg, Justice Arthur, 89, 90
Griswold v. Connecticut, 2, 58, 74, 83, 88, 117, 132

Harlan, Justice John Marshall, 83, 87–88, 90, 98, 116
harm principle
 exceptions to, 81
 and freedom of expression, 115–16
 meaning of harm, 78–79
 in Mill's thought, 77–81
Harper v. Virginia Board of Electors, 131
Hayek, F.A., 7, 27, 121
Hegel, Georg Wilhelm Friedrich, 12, 22, 37, 42, 50
Hobbes, Thomas, 28
Hobhouse, L.T., 4, 121
Holmes, Justice Oliver Wendell, Jr., 71
 equal protection, view of, 131
 and "fighting faiths," 109
 meets Mill, 108
 Mill's influence on, 3, 107–8
Humboldt, Wilhelm von, 34
 anti-moralism of, 37
 concept of self-individuation, 36
Hume, David, 31, 42, 44, 120, 122
Hustler Magazine v. Falwell, 118

innate differences, Mill's attack on the theory of, 128
innate principle metaphysics, 44
intuitionism, Mill's attack on, 23

Jackson, Justice Robert, 76, 112
Jefferson, Thomas, 28, 62, 105, 112

Kant, Immanuel, 35–36
Kennedy, Justice Anthony, 97, 99, 118

law *versus* liberty, Locke and Bentham's contrasting views on, 34
Lawrence v. Texas, 2, 58, 96, 97
Leibnitz, Gottfried Wilhelm, 35

liberal and conservative as political terms, first use of, 27
liberalism
  antipathy to custom and tradition, 45
  continental influence on, 34–37
  distinguished from classical political thought, 28–29
  essential attribute of, 28–29
  history of, 27–28
  Mill's influence on modern, 46–53
  and positivism, 43–44
libertarianism
  first expression of, 35
  Mill's, 49
liberty
  Mill's theory of, 1–3, 47–53
  negative and positive ideas of, 59
  three aspects in Mill's thought, 2–3
Lochner v. New York, 57, 71. *See also* freedom of contract
Locke, John, 27
  conservatism of, 31
  liberalism of, 29–31
  theory of natural rights, 30–31. *See also* natural law; natural rights
Loving v. Virginia, 95, 130

Magna Carta, 57
Marbury v. Madison, 57, 62, 63
Meyer v. Nebraska, 73, 87, 90, 94
Mill, Harriet Taylor, 1, 17
  character of, 14
  death of, 16
  influence on Mill, 17
Mill, James, 7, 8
  education of, 9
Mill, John Stuart
  ambivalent place in liberal tradition, 50
  character of, 18–20
  childhood and education, 7–11
  children, obligation to support, 135
  choice-making central to freedom, 46–47
  conception of freedom, 47–49. *See also* self-individuation
  on conservatism, 20
  contrast with progressive liberalism, 4
  criticism of republicanism, 59–60
  death of, 26
  early skepticism about utilitarianism, 12
  economic views, 52
  equality, view of, 122–24
  feminism and liberalism, connection between, 136
  feminism of, 3–4, 129–36
  as foundational thinker, 38–39
  freedom of expression as core aspect of freedom, 103
  freedom *versus* equality, 123–25
  history, view of, 50
  imperialism, views on, 23
  inductive empiricism of, 44
  innate differences, attack on, 128
  intuitionism, critique of, 45
  libertarian *versus* progressive tendencies, 49
  marriage to Harriet Taylor, 15–16
  meets Oliver Wendell Holmes, Jr., 107
  member of Parliament, 24–25
  nervous breakdown, 11
  opposition to custom and tradition, 45
  positions as Member of Parliament, 25
  positivism of, 43–45
  progressivism of, 50–53
  publications, 21–24
  qualitative utilitarianism of, 41
  racial injustice, attack on, 125–26
  reformer of the world, 10
  relationship with Harriet Taylor, 13–17
  relationship with parents, 8–9
  right to marry and divorce, 129
  secular thinker, 39
  slavery, attack on, 125
  socialist leanings, 50–52
  spends night in jail, 10
  three core aspects of liberty, 82
  view of Christianity, 39–40
  view of the just society, 22
Miller, Justice Samuel Freeman, 67, 68
Miller v. California, 115
Minor v. Happersett, 131
Moore v. East Cleveland, 94
moralism, 37, 79, 88
  Mill's critique of, 80–81
  and the right to privacy, 98–99
Muller v. Oregon, 73, 131

National Labor Relations Board v. Jones and Laughlin Steel, 76
natural law, 29, 30, 31, 34, 40, 44, 64
natural rights, 40
Nebbia v. New York, 75
negative liberty, 47, 59. *See also* classical liberalism
New York Times v. Sullivan, 117, 118, 119

Obergefeld v. Hodges, 58, 99
obscenity, 115. *See also* freedom of expression

Olmstead v. United States, 59, 82, 83, 85
On Liberty, 1
and Darwinianism, 49
immediate influence of, 16–17, 84

Pace v. Alabama, 130
Paris Adult Theatre I v. Slayton, 115
paternalism, 2, 32, 53, 79, 80, 81
Mill *versus* modern liberals on, 79–80
perfectibility of man, 35
Pierce v. Society of Sisters, 74, 87, 90
Plesy v. Ferguson, 130
Poe v. Ulman, 87
police power, 69–71, 98
poll taxes, unconstitutionality of, 131. *See also* *Harper v. Virginia Board of Electors*
polygamy, Mill's view of legal prohibition, 81
positive freedom and equality, 123
positivism, meaning of, 43–44
Principles of Political Economy, 17, 21, 51
Privileges or Immunities clause, 66, 67, 68, 69, 129, 131
procreation and gender inequality, 128
prostitution, 30, 45, 79, 80, 81, 96
Proudhon, Pierre-Josef, 12

race and the Supreme Court, 129–33
racial injustice, Mill's attack on, 125–26
Ralph Waldo Emerson, 42, 43, 107
Rawls, John, 38
Reed v. Reed, 133
Reid, Thomas, 23
religion, Mill's views on, 10
representative-to-constituent ratio, then and now, 61
republicanism
in American constitution, 60–63
versus liberalism, 59–60
Mill's criticism of, 59–60
right of self-ownership, 29, 80
right to be let alone, 82, 83, 84, 85, 89
right to die, 96
right to marry, 95
right to privacy, 82–94
right to procreate, 86
Roberts, Chief Justice John, 98–99
Roberts, Justice Owen, 75
Roe v. Wade, 58, 92, 95
romanticism, 12, 35, 37, 38, 41, 42, 43, 45, 46, 116
definition of, 42
influence on Mill, 11–13
Roosevelt, Franklin Delano, 75, 76, 86, 121
Rorty, Richard, 38
Rousseau, Jean-Jacques, 35, 42, 48, 60, 128
Russell, Bertrand, 26

Say, Jean-Baptiste, 9
Schenk v. United States, 108
secularism
in Bentham' thought, 33
in Mill's thought, 39
self-development, 2, 4, 12, 22, 26, 43, 46, 47, 48, 49, 79, 102, 103, 111, 123. *See also* self-individuation
self-individuation, 2, 40, 45, 52, 77, 102, 123
necessary condition for in Humboldt's thought, 36
self-regarding activities, 80
Shapiro v. Thompson, 132
Shelley, Percy, 42
Skinner v. Oklahoma, 86. *See also* right to procreate
Skokie v. National Socialist Party of America, 114
Slaughterhouse Cases, 66
slavery, Mill's attack on, 125
socialism, Mill's view of, 50–52
society as tyrant, 47–48
Spencer, Herbert, 18, 72, 99
St. Simon, 12
Stanton v. Stanton, 134
Stephens, Leslie, 22
Stolen Valor Act, 118
Strauder v. West Virginia, 130
Sturm und Drang, 35
Subjection of Women, 3, 17, 25, 123, 125, 127, 128, 129, 133, 134
Supremacy clause, 60
System of Logic, 15, 18, 21, 23, 38, 41, 44, 47, 107, 123, 128, 129, 136

Taney, Roger, 1
Terminello v. Chicago, 114
Thirteenth Amendment, 65
Tiedeman, Christopher, 70
Tocqueville, 1, 4
tyranny, 62
tyranny of the majority, 4, 47, 48, 59, 78, 103, 123

United States v. Alvarez, 118
United States v. Virginia, 134
utilitarianism, 7, 10, 12, 22, 24, 31, 32, 33, 35–36, 38, 40, 41, 43, 45, 107
influence on liberalism, 31–34
Mill's qualitative form of, 41
Mill's version of, 40–41
versus rights, 40

as secular foundation for politics and morality, 32
as threat to liberty, 33

Warren and Brandeis right to privacy article, 83–86
Washington v. Glucksburg, 96
welfare benefits, constitutional regulation of, 132
West Coast Hotel v. Parrish, 75
West Virginia State Board of Education v. Barnette, 76
Westminster Review, 10
Whitney v. California, 110
Wordsworth, William, 11, 12, 42

Yick Wo v. Hopkins, 130

Zablocki v. Redhail, 95, 135